THE
FIRST LADY

Darlene Grant

Gracefully Yours

Lyrics used in this Novel:
"Ordinary Just Won't Do"
Commissioned, Verity Records (2002).
"Peace of God" Tarralyn Ramsey, Verity Records (2002).
"There's Not a Friend Like the Lowly Jesus"
Lyrics by Johnson Oatman, Jr. (1856-1926).
"What Can Wash Away My Sins"
Lyrics by Robert Lowry (1826-1899).
"The Blood Will Never Lose Its Power"
Lyrics by Civilla D. Martin (1915 or earlier)

ISBN 978-0-615-35122-3
Printed in the United States

To my Mom, Mae.
You are a graceful woman of standard.
Thank you for the many sacrifices made.
I love you

ACKNOWLEDGEMENTS

To the generations of Valiant Men in my life:
Dad, Theodore Patten Sr., I miss you desperately. The work continues.
Grant, my love, thank you for unending support, undivided attention, and endless love.
Lloyd, Rick, Evan, and Ryan, thank you all just for being you. You all make being a Mom delightful.
T. Brown, your eye for detail and keen insight made this project possible. A. Hargrove and M. Gallagher, your assistance with the cover art was priceless. M. Garrott, thank you for listening to countless ideas for countless hours. To the women that read this manuscript and provided invaluable feedback, I am grateful. Merci.

To the readers...whatever situation you find yourselves in, take the time to look beyond what you see and remember conventional weapons and methods are useless against supernatural conflicts and struggles. You're a winner! Hone your spiritual fighting skills and remember who you are fighting.

When a trumpet sounds in a city, do not the people tremble? When disaster comes to a city, has not the Lord caused it? Surely the sovereign Lord does nothing without revealing his plan to his servants the prophets. The lion has roared who will not fear? The Sovereign Lord has spoken – who can but prophesy?

Amos 3:6-8

1

THE INTERCESSOR
1:30 AM

A luminous moon flourished against the clear, dark, star drizzled sky in the sixteen acre farming town of Lovett. Hints of farm animal aroma spiked the crisp November air of the close knit, slow paced community. After nine o'clock, Lovett showed no signs of life. The small pizza shop, the local hardware store, and the convenience store, in the center of town, shut down by sundown. The rural splendor of rolling fields flanked behind colorful, towering trees faded into the night. Outside of the occasional high beams of a wandering vehicle or nocturnal insect clatter, one could only see darkness and hear silence.

Lydia sat gazing out of her bedroom window. Feeling extremely heavy and sorrowful, she sat in the tattered recliner unable to sleep listening to the strangest thing…birds chattering back and forth.

The cheerful chatter prompted a smile. *How weird*, she mused, *given the time of morning.*

A staccato chirp, a returned whistle type chirp, followed by a rolling, high pitched chirp.

As the chatter subsided, Lydia finally began to doze. Labored breathing and eyes darting back and forth, she found herself in a very familiar place.

The grandeur of the historic building transformed into a hauntingly, repressed citadel. The high ceilings lined with beautiful cedar beams reaching towards its peak now appeared as warped limbs, barely able to point. Small wisps of vapor escaped from the once resplendent stained glass windows. A heavy coat of condensation concealed the room from all outside light. The rich, ornate woodwork that lined every wall was also covered with the heavy coat of condensation or was it slime? Through squinted eyes, Lydia wondered, *is the substance moving?*

Before she could get a closer look, a bitter cry pierced the oppressed atmosphere. A startled Lydia approached the altar. The cry became muffled. "I know that voice," Lydia muttered under her breath. "That looks like...oh my God."

A well dressed, medium form lay crumpled on the altar crying inconsolably. "Lord, what's wrong with her? What am I doing here?" Expecting no reply, Lydia allowed herself to absorb the full effect of the room. Dreaming, seeing (with spiritual eyes while awake), and knowing (the realization of the unseen) was not foreign to her. These gifts always reaffirmed her understanding of natural and supernatural life. There was always a purpose and a message.

Continuing her examination of the once exquisite sanctuary, Lydia began to hear the faint cries of others who lay prostrate in between pews and on the front altar. The escalation of weeping and moaning fused with sorrow and oppression produced an atmosphere thick enough to cut with a knife. The same sorrow and heaviness she carried for the past few days.

Feeling like she was suffocating, Lydia fell to her knees bent over with her arms wrapped around her stomach. Coughing, gagging and panting. Lydia could not breathe. A firm hand gently touched her shoulder and immediately her anguish subsided. Slowly and deliberately turning to see who touched her, Lydia stopped. Stricken with awe and amazement, she beheld a magnificent brilliance emanating from one spot.

A spectacular man stood before her with a stern demeanor and powerful presence exuding great calmness and comfort. Attempting to rise from her knees, Lydia's entire body trembled. She parted her lips to speak, however, no words surfaced. The desire to touch the man was overwhelming. *Is he real? Am I having a dream within a dream?* He was too beautiful to be real. Her gaze held by his brilliance, Lydia slowly stretched out her hand towards the man. The realization emerged. He is a Messenger sent to bring understanding to what she was seeing.

Before she could reach the tip of the Messenger's fingers, her attention was snatched by an image sitting in the corner, very relaxed, basking in the atmosphere.

Lydia could not make out any features; however, she knew the overwhelming essence of this place derived from this image.

The Messenger spoke, "That is the Spirit of Lust. He was invited into this place through deprivation and greed. Lust has taken the ordinary desires of many and multiplied them far beyond their natural tendencies. Now their desires, fueled by lustful imaginations, are being acted out in evil, sensual, and abominable acts. These you see weeping are sorely grieved and vexed for the abominations that are committed in this place."

The Messenger began to walk through the people strewn along the floor, Lydia followed. In the back of the sanctuary, they stopped at the first office. The sign on the huge mahogany door read *Pastor's Study*. Without knocking, the room opened to full view.

About thirty leaders stood in a circle; Pastors, Elders, Deacons, Teachers, and Ministers. In the middle of these leaders clothed in a radiant white robe trimmed in purple sat the Shepherd of the flock. While Lydia could not see his face, everything about him was very familiar. She uttered his name through partially closed lips.

The Shepherd engaged in a lewd act with a woman. Although each leader watched, they all had their own agendas concerning the woman. The woman seemed catatonic following the Shepherd's instructions dutifully and mechanically, as if she had no idea that she was being abused.

Lydia gasped, tears streaming down her cheeks. The Messenger proceeded to walk a few feet down a short corridor and stood in front of another door marked *Chapel*. This room, also in full view, was occupied by many women with connected hands surrounding a breathtaking, seven-foot-tall, voluptuously carved statue.

Focusing on the sculpted master piece, Lydia began to notice the striking details. Diamond tipped finger nails, toe nails adorned with sapphire, and the front of its torso a kaleidoscope of glistening emeralds, rubies, and amethyst. Its hair, fine, thin, strands of gold that seemed to slightly move from a gentle breeze. A thick, two-tone, gold braided chain held a flowing cape extending into a long train made of currency from several countries. Spotlights from different parts of the room drowned the image in glory. Monitors displayed the image which seemed to increase in size and stature with constant focus.

The Messenger spoke, "these weep not for the abominations done in the Father's house. They have a form of godliness, yet deny His power. These weep at the feet of their chosen deities: beauty, fame, and fortune, which they seek with their whole hearts."

The Messenger proceeded further down the corridor and stopped at two huge doors. The room opened to full view and Lydia saw children as young as ten and adults as old as seventy-five. Some cowered in corners as if being whipped while others glided around the room as if under the influence of some type of hallucinogen. Others sat in agitated states of jerking, scratching, and swatting at things that were not there. Lydia's heart began to ache at the zombie like states.

The Messenger spoke, "these are held captive through varied types of substances and substance abuse. Some are here through physician diagnosis and some through spiritual diagnosis believing in the maladies and prescriptions given them. Others voluntarily indulged in futile attempts to dull past pains and uncertain futures, and yet others, for sheer enjoyment and curiosity. The drugs, regardless of the reasons for use, were a portal for the spiritual entities that now torture them. Although you see this here, in this house, truly I tell you that these abominations have plagued many of the Father's houses around the world.

"See what the elders and leaders do in the dark? The way of the truth has been compromised. In their greed and sensuality, they have made up cleaver lies to get hold of people and money, but God has condemned them and destruction is on the way.

"Although the judgment of the Lord will come, and the people will be scattered, He will be to them as a little sanctuary in the place where they shall go.

"He that hath an ear let him hear what the spirit says to the church. The Sovereign God says, 'for I am the Lord: I will speak, and the word that I speak shall come to pass; it shall be no more prolonged. For in your days, oh rebellious house, will I say the word, and will perform it. For I know the things that come into your minds, every one of them. Why should you be beaten anymore? Ye will revolt more and more. The whole head is sick, and the whole heart is faint. From the sole of the foot, even unto the head, there is no soundness in it, but wounds, and bruises, and putrefying sores. They have not been closed, neither bound up, neither mollified with ointment. For the pastors have become senseless and do not inquire of the Lord; so they will not prosper and their flock shall be scattered. When they fast, I will not hear their cry; and when they bring their offerings, I will not accept them: but I will consume them with famine and deprivation. Yet it shall come to pass, after I have plucked them out, I will return, and have compassion on them, and will bring them again.' He that hath an ear, let him hear, what the spirit is saying to the church."

The Messenger stood near the entrance of the sanctuary with a clear view of the state before him. A loud, thunderous voice bellowed, "Cause the keepers of the state to draw near."

Five men stood around the perimeter of the State, each with a pen in his hand. The voice continued, "Go through the towns and put a mark on the foreheads of everyone who is in anguish over the outrageous obscenities being done in the State. At the set time, I will cause it to rain a grievous hail upon this place. Send and cause the righteous to flee into their homes that they may be spared." The keepers began at the House of God.

The keepers of the State returned and reported the matter saying, "We have done as commanded." Then the Lord sent peals of thunder and hail laced with lightning strikes.

2

A light rain pelted against the window and a damp chill seeped through microscopic cracks in the sill. Lydia bolted up in the bed, heart pounding and eyes darting about. Realizing that she lay in her bedroom, she placed her hand over her heart whispering, "Okay, okay, calm down." Her night shirt soaked in perspiration caused her to shiver and pull the blanket up to her neck tightly. Exhaling exhaustively, Lydia glanced at the clock with the thought of calling Helen, but at three o'clock in the morning, someone had better be dying. That was always their rule. "Someone is dying," she reasoned. "A whole lot of someones."

Before Helen became Mrs. Payton Roosevelt, then, First Lady Helen Roosevelt, she and Lydia were sisters. For a while, they were connected at the hip. However, as responsibilities grew for each of them, they saw less of each other, yet their relationship remained solid. They discussed any and everything. Regardless of the length of time between conversations, they would pick up from where they left off without missing a beat.

Falling back, allowing her head to sink into two fluffy pillows, Lydia reminisced; her personal relationship with God began when she met Helen.

Lydia sat at the hospital awaiting news regarding an intimate friend that she greatly loved. Her friend lay dying and she stood outside of the hospital room door falling apart inwardly. Leaning against the dingy, white wall to steady herself, the hallway seemed to close in, Lydia's mouth watered uncontrollably. The rumbling of her breakfast began a slow ascent to her esophagus. Forcing everything back down she groaned realizing that she was about to be sick.

Lydia could not remember where Helen had come from, but Helen gently touched Lydia's arm and said, "You look like you need to sit."

Hesitantly, Lydia complied for fear of fainting. They drank tea and talked feeling as if they'd known each other forever. Helen spoke kindly to Lydia, encouraging her to read Psalms to sooth her during her crying spells and anxiety.

Their talk turned into dinner, dinner turned into movies, aerobics, social events, and just tea. They found true sisterhood and identified each other in that manner from that point.

Determined to check in with Helen at first light, Lydia closed her eyes and asked the Lord to strengthen and keep Helen's heart and mind.

3

The warm, mid-day sun bathed the gardens in brilliance as mingling aromas collided creating pungent fragrances wafting in the breeze. Well-wishers, family members, and congregants sauntered from one food tent to the next inebriated by the countless delicacies from several countries.

Showcasing their multicultural ministries, Spirit and Truth Worship Center exuberantly celebrated twenty-five years of unwavering spiritual guidance in the community.

First Lady of Spirit and Truth Worship Center, Helen Roosevelt, drank in the moment. Her eyes shimmered as she watched the waves of people move from place to place. It was very seldom she was able to stand alone, anywhere, for any length of time, uninterrupted in her thoughts. Her head tilted back slightly, medium length soft curls dangling down her neck revealed a naturally pretty afro centric woman with dark chocolate skin, slender face, almond shaped eyes, high cheek bones, and full lips.

Adorned in a silk, tangerine, fitted sundress, Helen was radiant. Basking in the sun as she twirled her pearls around her fingers, Helen pondered their humble beginnings watching her husband, Pastor Payton Roosevelt, stroll from one group to the next flashing his pearly whites. Today, he reminded her of the young man she fell in love with twenty-seven years ago. Closing her eyes, she imagined herself engulfed in the aromatic atmosphere charged by his scent, embraced in strong, dark arms full of sensual messages.

Every soft touch emitted electrical current pleading to connect, to become one. He ravished her and every thought that desperately fought for her attention dissipated. One single thought melted into every crevice of her mind, "I love this man."

A light buzz in Helen's ear startled her out of her reverie. Flinching, she swatted the bug away and continued to observe the crowd, grateful and excited that they made it this far in ministry. The Roosevelts had so many friends with different ministries and churches that fell prey to scandalous events causing church splits, shut downs, and even divorce. By the grace of God, they were celebrating twenty-five years of ministry and twenty-seven years of marriage.

With her whole heart, Helen believed in Payton's ministry and call. He proved to be a man of character, integrity, and stability. "What more could a girl want? Baby, stay sincere," she whispered through her girlish smile while he made his way through the crowd toward her direction. Helen sat on a stone bench amidst a tapestry of foliage and flowers.

When Payton emerged from the thicket of people, Helen leaped up and threw her arms around his neck. "Hey baby," she purred. "You look so good today. I've been thinking about you all day. I miss you so much."

Payton nuzzled her neck. "Hey beautiful, I miss you too. Mmmmm, you are so soft."

"Don't start nothin' won't be nothin'." Helen giggled. "You were saying?"

"Oh yeah, you know you mess me up like that girl. Anyway, the hard part is over. We'll have our time after today."

"Oh, that's way too long. What do you say we sneak away for a few minutes?" Helen cooed as she raised one eyebrow slightly, "I need you."

Payton laughed out loud. "Don't tempt me. I might have to get on stage and deliver an early benediction. I'll tell you what. After our presentation, let's take a long walk and we'll handle that need."

She laughed, "Promises, promises." Grabbing his hands to keep them securely wrapped around her waist, Helen whispered lightly, "I am overwhelmed. Look at this. Is this really our ministry? Five nations represented. My cup runneth over. You are an amazing man."

"Hold that thought," Payton whispered and kissed her on the cheek. "I'll be right back."

"Payton, where are you? Wait!" Before Helen could get her words out, he rushed across the gardens onto the stage. Helen plopped on the bench, crossed her arms, and threw one leg over the other swinging it back and forth.

Maribel, one of the administrative assistants walked up. "What's going on with you? You look a little twisted, First Lady."

"Excuse me?" Helen answered irritably.

Maribel cocked her head to one side and sucked her teeth. "Aggravated, irritated, come on First Lady, you know what I mean. You look like somebody just stole something from you."

"Well, I guess you could say that. Anyway, it's not that important. How are you, Maribel?" Helen loved Maribel's thick Spanish accent. An attractive, fair skinned young lady, Maribel weighed one hundred ten pounds soaking wet.

"I'm okay," Maribel answered. "I saw you over here alone and thought I'd keep you company, but here comes a pack of rats."

First Lady snickered. "You know what Maribel, that's not very nice."

"Come on First Lady, they are so phony. They don't even like you. You know that right? Well, maybe not all of them, but that one in the middle really don't like you."

Swatting Maribel on the hip, Helen muttered, "Oh stop that and try to be cordial."

"Oh no, I can't take them. I'll say my goodbyes right now. You watch. One day you will come to me and say, Maribel, you were right."

"Remember Maribel, God loves everybody, even the phony folks."

"Si, adios First Lady. Yo le veré el lunes."

"English please."

"Sorry, I'll see you on Monday." Maribel whipped her wavy, black hair behind her as she profiled with hand on hip, contemplating the women approaching. "Hola chicas."

Michelle, Rachel, and Mia glanced as Michelle spoke for everyone. "Hello, Maribel, goodbye Maribel, you might as well keep walking."

Firing back with a litany of insults in Spanish, Maribel flipped her hair again and walked away.

Rachel raised her hands offering a half bow, "Hail, Oh Queen." Helen rolled her eyes and attempted to ignore the remark.

"Hi First Lady," Michelle and Mia sang together.

"Hey ladies," how are you?

Rachel harassed, "Oh, the Queen is not pleased today?"

"Rachel!" First Lady snapped, "Why must you be so irritating? I am not in the mood."

"Well, who yanked your chain?" Rachel responded sharply.

"You did, just now Rachel. That mouth. You never know what to say, do you?"

"Testy, testy are we? I'm just messing. What's going on with you?"

"I'm sorry; I guess I'm a little edgy. I need some sleep and a vacation."

"You deserve one too sweetie," Michelle replied. "You worked like a mad woman and to me, it was worth it."

Mia jumped in, "any event with free food is worth it for you Michelle. All you do is eat."

"Be quiet, Mia. I can't help it if that's my favorite pass time." They all laughed.

"Yes, it is," Rachel joined in. "Don't feed that girl and watch out. She's like a bear waking up from hibernation."

"Okay, that's enough," Michelle fussed as her face went solemn and broke out into laughter again.

Helen fingered her pearls. "So, what do you ladies really think of this grand event?"

Mia turned to First Lady, "You are a phenomenal woman. Really! I know that sounds so cliché, but to birth a magnificent idea and then bring it together with caring and personal touches speak volumes of your love for people. I don't think you left one stone unturned. Everything fits perfectly."

Michelle interrupted, "Well there's nothing more to be said. Miss mouth has voiced it all. By the way, thank you, Mia. I could not have said it better."

"Thank you all," Helen replied warmly. "Payton and I could not have done this without you. You all have played such an integral part in the ministry. Rachel, you've been with us for what, ten years?"

"Yup, and I'm not leaving until the Lord calls me home."

"Well that could be tomorrow hon, don't tempt Him," Michelle smirked with her nose drawn up.

Helen nudged Michelle's arm, "You and Mia are old timers being that you've been with us since the beginning."

Michelle, the tenacious, robust, six feet two inch, brown skinned Elder and Mia, the small, exotic,

Filipino beauty came to the ministry when the doors first opened through the different city wide youth rallies sponsored by the ministry. They grew into real spiritual jewels navigating murky waters with Helen over the years. Always her amen corner, Helen realized how blessed she was having these women by her side. Helen continued, "Your opinions mean a lot to me. Anyway, you guys have to help make sure everything runs smoothly over the next week. We're out of here and not a moment too soon."

Rachel's eyes widened. "What do you mean? Are you going somewhere?"

"Yes, we're going away for a little R and R. Not that we'll be doing that much sleeping," Helen smiled slyly.

Rachel whined, "How long will you be gone?"

"We will be gone for ten, spicy, hot days. Didn't you know? It's on the calendar."

"I did," Michelle interjected with her hand on her hip. "And so did Mia. Miss Thing here must be slipping."

"Well, now that everyone knows, handle it," Helen said light heartedly "I am out of here. Smooches."

Michelle and Mia blended into the crowd surrounding the stage as the upbeat Jamaican type lyrics rang out,

This is the day that the Lord has made. I will rejoice and be glad in it. This is the day that the Lord has made.

As people swayed and stepped to the music, Helen felt a slight tug in the pit of her stomach.

"Helen, wait up," Rachel squealed rushing to her side.

"I can't really. I'm about to be summoned. Enjoy the rest of the festivities."

"I'll walk with you," Rachel said nervously. "I need to see what Pastor wants me to do at the conclusion of the ceremony."

"What do you mean what he wants you to do? I thought you already went over that."

"Well you know he changes his mind like the weather. He told me to see him after the Jamaican presentations."

"What are you talking about, Rachel? He doesn't...never mind." Helen decided to let the comment ride. "Rachel, where is Ray? I haven't seen him all day."

"Girl, I don't know what's going on with Ray lately. He seems to be going through the change of life or something. One minute he's sweet, the next minute he's angry and agitated."

"Well, face it, Rachel, you hardly spend any time with him. What do you expect?"

"I expect a little support. We work for the same ministry. He knows what my job entails."

"Yes, he does and you know what his entails. You're his wife, Rachel. Don't get this all twisted."

"First Lady, you need to walk out of the stone ages. We are in the new millennium. I'm not, nor have I ever been that kind of woman. Ray knows that and he has to take me as I am."

"Alright, if you say so, I'll talk to you later. That's my cue."

The First Lady

Pastor Payton Roosevelt adorned his wife with accolades and praise before the crowd. Everyone applauded and cheered. He leaned into Helen, kissed her softly; they waved and exited the stage.

4

At the end of Main Street, also known as the Strip, past the town hall and The Second Chance Rehab Center, stood the imposing Spirit and Truth Worship Center.

Sitting on five acres of land, the historic landmark welcomed passers-by with a weekly billboard message. This week's message: *Life is fragile, handle with prayer*. Listed in bold black letters under the weekly message was the service schedule and *Payton Roosevelt, Senior Pastor*. The restored sandstone, Gothic Cathedral with its 200 feet spire, beautiful columns, and painted arches sat loftily among a collage of trees and exotic foliage. An enormous, round, stained glass window that captured the sun and filtered a kaleidoscope of color into the sanctuary was the pride of the congregation. The lobby, outfitted with six feet columns, always bedecked with fresh flowers and an information table, separated from the sanctuary by two, ornately carved, swinging double doors with stained glass panels.

The cavernous sanctuary, a masterpiece of delicately sculpted gothic forms, included painted arches and pinnacles. A soaring ceiling lined with beautiful cedar beams reaching towards its peak, resplendent stained glass windows and rich, ornate woodwork surfaced every wall. A marble pulpit exquisitely carved with angelic figures interspersed with scriptural calligraphy adorned the center front of the sanctuary.

The church ran like a well-oiled machine, everyone and everything in their respective places. Assistant Pastor Raymond Morgan, Director of the Elders, Deacons, and Ministers; Elder Michelle Mitchell, Director of Community Outreach; Sister Mia Robbins, Director of Administration; Minister Rachel Morgan, Director of the Church Counselors/Social workers and wife of Assistant Pastor Raymond Morgan; Mother Eleanor Corbett, Director of the Benevolence Ministry; and Elder Darnell Harris, Director of the Youth Ministries. There was also a Sunday School Superintendent; Special Events Coordinator; Intercessory Prayer Director and Team; Minister of Music; Adult, Young Adult, and Children's Choirs; Praise Dancers, and Drama Club. Everything seemed to run smoothly, until today.

Raymond Morgan, a burly, six feet, four-inch line-backer type with vanilla complexion, a square jaw and a clef in his chin. He'd been with the ministry for twenty years and the Assistant Pastor for fifteen. Ray was very impressed with the young visionary he'd met on the college campus at the opposite end of town twenty some years ago during a youth rally. Pastor

Roosevelt was on fire for the Lord. He persuaded
hundreds of students to take on Christianity as a
lifestyle. His vision, confidence, and sincerity won
Ray's vote. Ray never questioned his Pastor's motives
or decisions. If Pastor Roosevelt said it, it was as good
as done. Everything he touched, everything he spoke
about turned into success. However, over the past five
years, Ray began to notice subtle changes in the man of
God he served with for so long. Even now, Ray would
not question or comment on what he saw, he just
prayed.

Today, unlike any other day, Ray sat in his office
gazing upon the manila envelope resting on his desk.
The contents stripped him of his dignity and self-
respect. Hadn't he prayed that the Holy Spirit would
convict Payton?

Should he call their business partners? What if no
one knew what was happening? He didn't even know
what was happening yet. The church's alliance and
partnerships with Pastor Janardhin Muralitharan of
Bangalore, India; Pastor Mustapha Joloff of Senegal;
Pastor Antonio Quinones of Puerto Rico; and Pastor
James Allen of the local Full Gospel Church, were solid.
They formed an alliance known as *The Kingdom*,
approximately seven years ago. After much sacrifice,
investing, and selling their ideas, The Kingdom finally
had the monetary backing to do what they wanted:
television broadcasting, their own air transportation
and community redevelopment in each of the church's
territories. Now this!

The squeaking hinges of the door seized Ray's attention. Maribel's thick, Spanish accent sang a joyful greeting. "Hello, Pastor Ray. How you doing today? I'm sorry to bother you, but your wife wants to see you."

"Okay Maribel, please let her know that I'll be over in a few minutes." Still distracted by the envelope, Ray muttered to himself, "What in God's name is happening? How did I miss all of this?" He shifted in his chair as uneasiness massaged his temples. He tapped the intercom button, "Maribel, would you get the accountant on the phone?"

"Right away," she replied punching numbers into the telephone. "Feldman is on line two, Pastor Ray."

After an hour conversation, Ray leaned back in his chair and prayed. He exhaled sharply, "Maribel, I'm expecting a messenger to deliver a package here by 4:30 pm. If I'm not here, just hold on to it until I return."

5

Rachel Morgan was by no means an attractive woman, but there was something appealing about her that grabbed your attention. Besides the huge nose that was the focal point of her face and her large feet, the five feet, five inches, medium build, extremely outspoken, Rachel Morgan was resourceful, creative, and calculating. When her husband of six years waltzed into her office without knocking, she shot him a look. "Hey, this is a business. What happened to knocking and why did it take you so long?"

Ignoring his wife, Raymond picked Rachel up from the chair embracing her gently. "Did someone wake up on the wrong side of the bed this morning?"

"No! Please put me down. You're always acting like some kind of Neanderthal." Straightening out her clothes, Rachel irritably continued. "I need you to sign off on a few things before I run downtown. I have four people entering rehab today and I know I won't make it back before you leave."

"Sure thing honey, whatever you want." Ray's eyes sparkled as he admired the silhouette of her medium frame in the powdery blue, silk pants suit. She'd been spending so much time in the office; they were like two ships passing in the night.

"How about getting together this evening? I'd like to spend some time with my wife."

"Oooh, I'm sorry, sweetheart. Can I take a rain check? I'm supposed to meet with Pastor tonight at eight. He's returning from vacation and wants to make sure the paper work for the clinic on wheels is complete. We're supposed to go live tomorrow."

"Rachel, Pastor will understand. You can handle that tomorrow. You're very efficient, I'm sure everything is in place and ready to go. I suggest you call Pastor and let him know you won't be available tonight."

"Excuse me? I don't tell you how to handle your job, so please don't tell me how to handle mine. This is very important to me Raymond. Instead of your constant demands, I could use your support."

"Rachel, I'm going to say this once. You need to know when to cut things off. You're like a never ending story with everything but me. What's happened to you?"

"Nothing has happened to me. I just happen to like my job and I take it very seriously."

"Well take this seriously. Your husband and your home are first. If you don't get things in order, I'll do it for you. Consider this a warning because the next time we have a conversation like this, you won't have a job."

Before Rachel could respond, Ray was out the door. Steam seeped through every orifice on her face. She sat down at her computer and clicked her mouse on the icon in the right hand corner of the computer. She grumbled to herself, "Calm down. He's upset because he knows he doesn't matter." She'd already consulted her two books of wisdom this morning. "Let me make sure everything lines up." The window on her computer opened up to the horoscope page. Her horoscope read:

Today you'll have dual needs. On one hand, you'll want to take part in social activities. And at the same time, you'll need some time alone. Fortunately, you can and should do both! Today plan time with others, and also try to find someplace quiet where you can spend an hour alone.

"Excellent," Rachel exhaled. "I'll do just that, social time and time for myself and no one else. Raymond Anthony Morgan, you're on your own."

Rachel, always the consummate thinker, especially when it pertained to what she wanted, knew she needed to do something about her husband. As sweet as he could be, he was becoming a little too cocky lately demanding her time and attention. Retrieving the spare key to Ray's office, Rachel unlocked the door and walked in just as the messenger was delivering the expected package to Maribel's desk.

Normally Maribel would have slid the package under the door or dropped it in Ray's mailbox, but she did as she was told and held on to it. Rachel was in and out, quickly copying files and replacing them. Maribel watched the entire time as her fingers flew across the keyboard as if busying herself with correspondence. She never liked Minister Morgan. With a scowl on her face, she thought, *what does Pastor Ray see in her? She's so....so....evil.*

Ray breezed in and attempted to unlock his office door. Alarmed that it was already open, he walked over to Maribel with a perplexed look on his face speaking in a low tone, "who unlocked my office?"

"Your wife did. She was in there rummaging through your files, took three folders, copied them, and put them back. I'm not sure which folders."

"Maribel, look at me." His voice in a whisper, "where is my package?" Unsure why they were whispering, Maribel followed suit and mouthed, "Right here in my desk."

"Good girl," he smiled. Maribel shrugged her shoulders, trailed off into a Spanish discourse and passed him the package.

Ray marched into his wife's office, "what were you doing in my office Rachel?"

"Whatever do you mean Payton?"

"What did you just call me?!" His eyes began to bulge, "Did you just call me Payton?"

"Really Raymond, I was being snide with you, yanking your chain. You know I always say you should be the Pastor, not the assistant. Lighten up." She walked over to the door, stood on the tips of her toes and placed her arm around his neck trying to coax him through the door. "I'm sorry about my attitude earlier." She kissed his lips. "I'll make it up to you, okay. And, to answer your question, I needed the minutes from the last few staff meetings."

"You could have gotten that information from Mia or Maribel."

"I don't like asking them for anything. Why don't you want me in your office, Ray? I'm your wife. Are you hiding something?" She stroked the back of his neck, "are you?"

"No Rachel! Just don't unlock my office for any reason when I'm not here. Understand?"

"Fine, fine, have it your way, big guy. Now, about making up," she whispered reaching around his waist pulling him all the way inside of the office and closing the door.

6

The atmosphere was electric. Sporadic outbursts of praise collided with the whine of the organ. *"Hallelujah, glory to God, glory to your name, Jesus."*

After a litany of approbation, the Worship leader bellowed, "LORD YOU ARE GOOD! LORD, YOU ARE GOOD! LORD, YOU ARE GOOD...AND YOUR MERCY ENDURES FOREVER!" An eruption of applause accompanied by an instrumental explosion filled the sanctuary. The praise escalated. Singers sang, *'You are good, all the time, all the time, you are good.'* Some of the congregants jumped up and down, some danced while others raised their hands and lifted their heads towards the sky. Everyone rejoiced!

The First Lady sat on the front row in a high back, royal blue cushioned chair donned in a wide brimmed black Hat outfitted with ostrich feathers. A tapered, one button, single breasted, black coat dress trimmed in white and black, four inch pumps with a white tipped toe.

Helen sat very poised and deliberate which was highly unusual; however, her heart and feet were heavy. She couldn't fight past her pain. The beat of the drums seemed to mingle with the pounding against her chest. She screamed on the inside, "God why, why, why?!"

Strapped to the chair by malaise and nausea, Helen did not notice her husband enter the pulpit. The moment she saw his face, she wanted to heave but fought the urge. The very sight of Payton Roosevelt made her sick. "I hate you," she whispered through partially closed lips. "I don't even know who you are."

Pastor Roosevelt began the customary Sunday morning invocation in a rich, eloquent appeal. For a moment, she saw the man she admired and adored, dark, robust, and extremely handsome. His face outlined with thick eyebrows, full lips, and knowing eyes could almost take her breath away. The slight gray mingled in his sideburns gave him a look of distinction. However, already taken hostage by her thoughts, Helen jolted back into her feelings of hostility.

Helen mustered every ounce of strength to stand for the Morning Prayer. As the congregation worshipped, she could not imagine sitting through any more of the service, let alone Payton's sermon.

Heads bowed and eyes closed, Helen made a dash for the side door, nearly mowing down an old, tattered, vagabond hobbling towards the entrance. "I'm sorry," she whimpered scurrying off without hearing his response.

Payton stood in the pulpit delivering an astounding word of truth. Deep down in the crevices of his soul, he felt the rumbling of a volcano on the verge of eruption. Searching desperately for his wife, Payton had not seen Helen exit after the Morning Prayer. Her chair was empty. He knew it was ludicrous to expect a message through one of the ushers. Her eyes were empty. She was despondent. No words, no emotion, nothing. He would have felt better if she ranted and raved like a maniac. If she threw ugly insults or hit him, but nothing. Not one peep since that night.

Payton could feel the intense heat coursing from the small of his back up to the nape of neck; his legs seemed to rock and reel. *No! I am in control,* he thought. With that, the conclusion of his message erupted from his belly with great strength and authority. "...We will not fear, though the earth be removed, and though the mountains be carried into the midst of the sea, though the waters roar and be troubled and the mountains shake, God is in the midst of her. God is in the midst of us and we shall not be moved. Let the heathen rage, we shall not be moved. For by Him, we have run through troops; by our God, we have leaped over walls. So, I am persuaded that He is able to keep that which we have committed unto Him against that day. Are you persuaded? Are you......persuaded?"

He motioned for Pastor Ray Morgan, his Assistant Pastor, to take over the remainder of the service. Pastor Roosevelt concluded with, "The Altar is Open!" Dripping from head to toe, he slowly turned from the pulpit toward his chair. Every ounce of his energy dissipated like vapor rising from hot rocks suddenly doused with water as the organist played...

'Oh Peace of God, reign on me, my spirit's calling to be free. My heart is heavy, I'm weighted down, for I know that your presence will always be around. For the Peace of God surpasses all understanding.'

Pastor Morgan continued the Altar call. "Are you persuaded that the Almighty God is able? He knows all, He sees all, and He understands...ALL! There is nothing...no situation, no person, no thing, too hard for God. Allow Him to direct you, to comfort you, to speak peace to your soul today. Allow the Lord to change you in the midst of your situation, even if your situation doesn't change."

Pastor Roosevelt dropped to his knees with great force causing his jaws to jiggle and his teeth to clench together. He felt like a wet dish rag, wrung until there was nothing left. He mumbled under his breath, "God, did I lose her? Please, please, let her be home when I get there." As his quorum of Elders stood around him praying, he heard no answer, he felt no peace.

Rising to sit in his chair, his adjutant gave him a glass of orange juice and whispered in his ear, "What a word, Pastor. The Lord used you."

Payton half smiled and said, "To God be the glory." Normally the orange juice made him feel refreshed and a little less depleted. However today it was wet and rancid.

Glancing across the congregation of more than seven hundred people, his mind began to run rampant. The onslaught of questions that battered his brain caused his shoulders to slump and his already tired demeanor to diminish into a sick, foreboding gaze.

Unaware that he was no longer sweating, he took his cloth and wiped his face and neck as if some of the anxiety that surged into his spirit would recede.

Pastor Ray Morgan's voice broke into his thoughts, "Final words and benediction by our Pastor." Payton motioned for him to dismiss the service. "Everyone standing. Now unto Him, that is able to keep us from falling and to present us faultless before the presence of His glory with exceeding joy. To the only wise God our Saviour, be glory and majesty, dominion and power, both now and ever, amen."

Raymond embraced Payton, "Powerful word today, Pastor. Are you feeling okay?"

"Fine, fine...nothing a long nap can't cure. I haven't had much sleep in the past few days. Think you can take care of things around here?"

"Sure, no problem," Ray replied. "Would you like someone to drive you home?"

"Nah, that's not necessary. Thanks though, you be blessed."

"You too Pastor."

Purposely not changing his sweaty clothes worked to Payton's advantage in making a quick exit. As he passed through the sea of people drifting between his office and the pulpit, he readied his smile. "Hello, ladies," speaking to the church mothers. "You all look splendid as always."

They all chimed in, "thank you, Pastor."

"That was some word today," Mother Moore said as she pulled at his collar.

Mother James interjected before Mother Moore could finish, "Yes it was. You tell First Lady that I said to make sure she takes care of you. After a sermon like that, you need a good solid meal."

Mother Corbett interrupted, "She doesn't always have time to cook like that. You have her call me and I'll bring dinner over. I was going to speak with her after service today, but she left early."

Hugging each of them, "I'll give her the message. Thank you, mothers, now if you all will excuse me, I need to get out of these wet clothes." Before he turned to continue wading through the sea of people, he noticed Rachel walking toward his direction with a look of desperation plastered on her face. *No,* he thought, *not here, not today.*

Payton turned, smiled and waved his way through the congregation until he reached the door to his office.

Rachel determinedly pressed through the crowd toward the Pastor. Mother Moore leaned into the group of mothers, "There is somethin' with that young lady. Somethin' ain't right!"

"Heads up ladies, its praying time," Mother Corbett instructed. "Lock and load this Tuesday, twelve noon, no exceptions and no excuses."

With a deep sigh of relief, Payton locked the heavy door, walked into the bathroom and stepped in the shower. Dread began to run its course with every sprinkle that trickled down his body. The agonizing ache caused him to stop and allow the water to virtually wash the dread down the drain; however, it continually resurfaced like vicious waves before a storm. As he stood bracing himself against the black marble wall, he heard an old familiar song echoing in his mind.

'*What can wash away my sins? Nothing but the blood of Jesus. What can make me whole again? Nothing but the blood of Jesus. Oh precious is the flow, that makes me white as snow. No other fount I know, nothing but the blood of Jesus.*'

As the song rang out in his mind, over and over again, he began to reflect on what now seemed to be one of the most repulsive moments he ever encountered. *Funny*, he thought. *One minute the thrill and ecstasy felt so strong, it snatched his soundness. The next, everything attached to the situation turned into a stomach wrenching ache and stench that could not be washed away.*

The water continued to drip from the top of Payton's head. His mind raced to the first infamous encounter that catapulted his existence into a cataclysmic nightmare.

7

Helen couldn't remember how she made it home, however, parked in front of her garage door proved she drove from one destination to the next. Frozen to the steering wheel of her black Jaguar, she breathed a long sigh and began to cry, "God I don't know what to do! How could you allow this to happen?"

Shaking uncontrollably for what seemed to be a life time she whispered, "Help me, please." Helen coaxed herself out of the car to unlock the front door of what used to be a familiar place.

Every movement and gesture became mechanical as if someone switched Helen on auto pilot. Approaching her bedroom door, she hesitated. Her heart began to throb once again as she slipped down the hallway wall. "I feel like I'm dying. I've given my whole life to you Payton! Is this what I get in return? Ahhhhhhhhh, you #@%#&$%, I hate you," she screamed.

Recently, Helen began to question Payton's many late night and early morning Prayer vigils. She never thought he would use the altar as a cover for his detestable indiscretions.

"How could you?" Helen said softly, tilting her head to one side as if looking in Payton's face. "How, in God's name, could you give so much insight with such authority while living such a lie?" Helen tried to block the invasion of vivid images that stripped her of her dignity and self-esteem, but her attempts were futile.

After several deep breaths, Helen scrambled to her feet and hesitantly entered the bedroom. Stumbling through the door blinded by tears, Helen's heart stopped. With painstaking details, she remembered how much time they put into choosing just the right type of furniture for what they called their 'Haven'.

The room was comfortable and elegant with intricately carved, rich, woods and a beautiful, Persian rug. Commentaries lay scattered along Payton's bedside awaiting his return for the nightly reading rendezvous. Drinking in every detail, Helen sighed heavily, "what happened? What did I do wrong?"

Mentally walking through the rest of her house, Helen reminisced about how they debated over the round gilded mirror floating over the server in the dining room adorned by the elongated, antique bronze sconces. "I won that round," she said as she smiled to herself.

Pacing back and forth, she caught a glimpse of herself in the huge floor mirror. "Who are you?" She asked. Everyone had always complimented her as being attractive, classy, stylish and refined. "What happened to you? You can't even make a rational decision. How pathetic," she grimaced. "You don't have any answers now do you? You've put together an impeccable house. You've flawlessly entertained hundreds of the congregation and out of town guests, and tirelessly wrestled with noticeable advances and attempts towards your husband. Hmm, that sounds so gracious. Is that what you did? Well, I think you turned the other cheek just a little too much. You turned your head, your eyes, shucks; you were dog gone near blind."

Helen continued to study herself tracing the barely there lines in her face with her index finger. Her defined arms and legs gave her the appearance of being athletic; however, she hadn't done anything sports like since college. "I can't say it's because you look bad. There has to be some superficial, absurdly ridiculous reason. God! My whole life…wasted!"

"Helen," she spoke to herself slowly and deliberately. "Take yourself somewhere and think this through. Don't be stupid. You have no job; you have no income. Your entire life is tied into that man, this house and the ministry. Don't be hasty, right? Right! That sounds right. I'll take a ride and clear my mind. Things will look better in the morning." She burst into an uncontrollable laugh which instantly became a gut wrenching wail.

8

Lydia sat at the wrought iron Bistro table in her quaint, comfortable, Old World kitchen, clutching a cup of hot tea in both hands. Some months passed since that night, dreaming about Payton and Helen. She had been fasting and praying but today, for some reason, the burden was as heavy as the night she had the dream. She'd spoken with Helen several times and everything seemed right with her world.

Lifting the cup to her lips, Lydia allowed the warmth of the hot liquid to radiate through her fingers, calming the slight tremble that she could not seem to still. Brushing her thin, auburn hair away from her large greenish blue eyes, she thought, *I have to go see Helen. I need to see her face and look into her eyes.*

Still bewildered and nauseous, her small frame shuddered. Lydia staggered to the bathroom for a cool cloth to put on her aching head before lying across the bed releasing a low groan. "Lord, you always confirm through your word, but right now, I am so tired, I need some sleep."

The night before Lydia tossed and turned most of the night. Today, after an earlier cat nap, then watching the clock flip from one minute to the next, she realized that she was not going to get any sleep.

Lydia picked up her Bible and read the first scripture she opened to Jeremiah 7 chapter…

1 This is the word that came to Jeremiah from the LORD: 2 Stand at the gate of the LORD's house and there proclaim this message: Hear the word of the LORD, all you people of Judah who come through these gates to worship the LORD. 3 This is what the LORD Almighty, the God of Israel, says: Reform your ways and your actions, and I will let you live in this place. 4 Do not trust in deceptive words and say, this is the temple of the LORD, the temple of the LORD, the temple of the LORD! 5 If you really change your ways and your actions and deal with each other justly, 6 if you do not oppress the alien, the fatherless or the widow and do not shed innocent blood in this place, and if you do not follow other gods to your own harm, 7 then I will let you live in this place, in the land I gave your forefathers forever and ever. 8 But look, you are trusting in deceptive words that are worthless. 9 Will you steal and murder, commit adultery and perjury, burn incense to Baal and follow other gods you have not known, 10 and then come and stand before me in this house, which bears my Name, and say, we are safe - safe to do all these detestable things? 11 Has this house, which bears my Name, become a den of robbers to you? But I have been watching! declares the LORD.

Lydia laid the Bible down. "Lord," she paused to gather her thoughts. Noticing the tremble still in her hands, she grabbed her left hand with the right and began to wring them. The tremble began to spread to her arms and she began rocking back and forth.

"My mind can't seem to grasp the reality or enormity of what's happening." She let out a long, slow sigh and laid back on her pillows. Waiting in silence, Lydia grabbed her journal and began to write. She was sure of what she saw and sure of what was going to come to pass. Now, this evening she was sure that there was nothing she could do. God's judgment was certain. Finishing her thoughts, Lydia laid the journal on the nightstand, made a mental note to visit Helen and fell into a sound sleep.

9

Helen drove for nearly two hours. The intrusive beeping of the cell phone jolted her back from a despondent state. She did not remember driving this far, however, she fled to the only place she believed would offer her a moment of solace. Approaching the last exit on the expressway relieved some of the tension in her shoulders. Passing the Marina, Helen inhaled the fresh sea air as she escaped into her very own Norman Rockwell Masterpiece.

Sea Port, an alluring seaside full of Victorian charm and splendor with an unspoken proclamation of a time fondly thought of and untainted by materialistic fascination. The Port fostered a tranquil atmosphere for families to rediscover the lost art of conversation, relishing thoughts, dreams, and expectations.

Helen sailed down Beach Avenue towards the Cove watching the ocean spit and lash out against the rocks. Strangely unpopulated, Helen was grateful that she would not have to compete with the normal beach activity. Outside of the two young men dressed in wet suits with surf boards ferociously paddling towards their next great wave ride, the water was empty.

Helen sat gazing at the horizon, watching the seagulls fly against the wind, gliding and then diving for the catch. She knew she was ridiculously overdressed. "Who cares," she smirked removing her shoes and pantyhose before stepping out into the cool, damp sand. She wrestled with her chair and blanket before ripping them free from the trunk. With the final tug, it suddenly hit, *what are you doing?* Subconsciously, she whispered, "I don't know. I don't know what to do."

Helen plopped into her chair a few feet away from the ocean line and wrapped the small blanket securely around her arms. The rhythm and crash of the waves began to dissolve her mountain of emotions. She had not really eaten or slept for a few days as the vivid images in her mind transformed themselves into erotic scenes, each embellished greater than the first.

"So many revivals and prayer vigils, how many were genuine?" Her mind searched frantically for an answer. One single note of pure agony escaped from her lips as the flood gates of a well-built dam suddenly crashed into bitter weeping. The meandering pain that passed through every crevice in her soul finally reached its peak. Up until today, she'd been anesthetized. She wanted to respond, she wanted to rip the house apart, but she could barely get out of bed.

This was like a dream of her falling, never hitting bottom until now.

Today in the midst of the praising and the dancing in the sanctuary and now sitting on the beach, in the midst of the sun and water dancing along the shore line, she hit bottom with brute force. How could anyone ever endure such pain? Everyone seemed so jubilant while her own life imploded in one fail swoop.

Contemplating her demise seemed light compared to the pain and turmoil that now infected her total being. There would be no objection on her part if some major catastrophe just happened to snuff her out right now. At least she would have peace.

"God, I just want to die." Rocking back and forth with her face hidden from the sun, "I can't do it! I can't go back."

Helen's mind drifted to that horrible night. She called her daughter, Denise, living overseas with her Missionary husband, Stefon and their eighteen-month old daughter, Dana.

"Hi Nesy, I called to tell you that I love and miss you and the baby. How is everything?"

"Besides missing you and daddy, we're fine. Mommy, you sound uneasy, I should be asking you if you're okay." Nesy replied with a hint of worry in her voice.

"Oh, I'm fine. I just can't sleep."

"Where's daddy?"

"He's at prayer."

"Oh! Well, give him a big hug and kiss for me. We're looking to come home in a few months so stop being a worry

wart and try to get some sleep. I love you, Mommy. I'll talk to you soon."

"Okay sweetheart, kiss the baby for me and tell Stefon I said hello." Helen tried to soothe herself with hot tea. Her words "he's at prayer," consistently pricked her thoughts. "Maybe something's wrong," she pondered. "No, it's me...maybe not." Helen went back and forth with herself for a good half hour before deciding to ride down to the church.

"Maybe sitting on the altar will help me find out what's plaguing me."

Helen slowed to a crawl just before the expressway exit. Traffic was backed up for miles. This was not out of the ordinary if there was an accident or concert down at the beach. With that, she avoided the exit and decided to take back roads. She hated taking the back roads in the wee hours of the morning. The darkness was haunting.

Helen approached a stop light at a well-lit intersection. The scarce signs of life were a relief. She noticed a black Land Rover at the gas station across the street. "Hmmm, that looks like Payton's truck."

She watched the man get out of his truck to keep an eye on the gas meter. Helen's eyes lit and she muttered, "Hey handsome, what are you doing here?" Well engrossed in her thoughts, Helen missed the light as it turned back to red. "Oooohhhh, I'm glad there's no one behind me." Stuffing her hand in her pocketbook to find her cell phone, she almost missed the light again.

Helen sped across the intersection in an attempt to catch Payton. He took an unexpected turn. "This isn't the way home or to church. Where are you going this time of the morning?" Curiosity began getting the best of her.

Payton finally turned into a small, well-manicured, development. "Who in the world are you visiting at this hour?" There was nothing familiar about the neighborhood, but Payton was involved in so many projects with so many people, anything was probable. "There are no meetings going on this time of the morning. Where in God's name are you going?"

Payton approached what seemed to be a newly constructed carriage house. The garage door ascended and he drove inside. Helen's heart pounded violently, she stuttered, "What? What is this? What are you doing?"

Her mind raced wildly trying to extinguish the rapid fire consuming every rational thought. There has to be a reasonable explanation. Unbuckling her seat belt, Helen attempted to get out and knock on the door, but she could not move. She sat across the street, frozen to her seat, grappling with her thoughts. Grabbing the cell phone, she punched in Lydia's number then quickly hit the end call button on the phone. "I'll wait," she whispered. "As long as it takes, I'll wait."

1:22 am, Helen sat wide eyed and parched as if she had a hand full of cotton stuffed into her mouth. 2:30 am, the garage door began to rise and Helen's stomach twisted into hundreds of little knots. Two pairs of feet, one of them in dark, fluffy footies, appeared. The ascension of the garage door continued, horror gripped Helen's heart as Payton embraced......"Oh my God!"

Helen jumped out of her car and ran across the street to the garage. "What in the #%@# are you doing? What is this?" Her entire body shook uncontrollably.

"Helen," Payton jumped, totally alarmed and off guard, "What? How? This is not what you think!"

The woman began to back up slowly. "Helen, I'm sorry, please, it's not what you're thinking."

"Oh really! What am I thinking, you #@%&##! Why my husband has spent the last hour at your house, or someone's house. Whose house is this!!!? Maybe I'm thinking that I should just shoot you both."

"Helen, don't be ludicrous," Payton laughed nervously as he walked slowly towards her direction not knowing what was in her pockets.

"Don't move another step you #@$%#@! I guess this is your altar now? This is how you spend time with God?"

"Helen, I...."

"SHUT UP! Just shut up, Payton! How could you!" Almost instantaneously, she stopped ranting.
In one single movement, Helen slapped Payton's face so hard stars popped around his left eye. Her shoulders slumped, and she methodically turned and walked away.

Helen could not grasp words or feelings, only numbness. Screeching away from the curb, she pulled around the corner and parked. Tremors consumed her entire body. Hyperventilating and light headed, barely able to get the car door ajar, Helen leaned between the door and the car and heaved until there was nothing left in her.

10

Eleven pm, Helen pulled into the garage. The house dark and silent, she tried to allow herself a moment to adjust to the darkness. Feeling for the light switch, a soft touch brushed against her cheek.

"Payton!"

"I didn't mean to frighten you, Helen. Can we talk?"

"No, I'm tired," Helen replied sharply.

"Helen, please, I need you to……"

"You need? You have the audacity to say, you need? I think you've had an overabundance of what you need."

A deflated Payton slowly walked along the wall into the family room and sank onto the sofa in slow motion like a rag doll. The darkness seemed to be a presence and the silence seemed to creep about the room like a suffocating cloud of smoke. Constantly rubbing his large hand over his head, Payton Roosevelt, for the first time realized that he was lost. He winced repeatedly with his head resting in the palms of his hands as he recalled the women, the properties, and the money. How would he ever be able to explain himself to anybody, let alone his wife?

"God, what have I done?" He whispered over and over again. "How do I fix this? Lord, what do I need to do?"

He recalled one of his encounters: thrill, fear, excitement, panic, and ecstasy all at the same time.... laced with God's mercy. He remained unscathed, still able to preach the Word of the Lord with power and might. He knew he was wrong and his love for God had not changed, but the cravings always won out and God's grace always seemed to cover him.

Now, he felt like a kid playing in the ocean, subtly drifting away, losing sight of the shore line. He was in so deep, he was drowning and there was no one to save him because no one realized how far he'd gone.

Suddenly Payton jumped straight up off of the sofa, alarmed by the slight vibration in his pant pocket. His heart beating a hundred miles a minute, he fidgeted with retrieving the phone as if someone else could hear the vibration. The text message was short and lusty signed with a single letter, *A*.

11

Rachel sat in her office pensive and uneasy contemplating cancelling her appointments for the day. Seven years serving the church as a Counselor/Social Worker and Director and look at the mess she created. *This is sloppy* she thought.

The intercom broke into her thoughts, "your nine thirty is here."

Rachel gasped and uttered under her breath, "dog gone it, I totally forgot." She hit the intercom button, "Maribel, I need to reschedule. Please come in here for a moment."

"Sure thing, Minister Morgan."

"Who is it?"

"Rashon Davenport and he really don't look too good. You're supposed to send him to a 30-day program today."

Rachel put her hand on her forehead, "Oh my goodness, I seriously forgot. Call this number for me and ask for Sharon. She'll know what to do. Send

Rashon directly to her office and tell him that I have an emergency and will follow up with him in a few days."

"Ok, will do. Are you okay, you seem really frazzled today, *Mommie*."

"Yeah, well, I'm not your concern. Just do your job, and don't call me *Mommie*."

Maribel sucked her teeth, "fine, suit yourself." As Maribel began her rescheduling duties, she felt the breeze from the passerby. "Good morn... Coffee? Tea? Guess not," Maribel snuffed.

The door opened to Rachel's office and she shot a stream of insults towards the intruder. "What are you an idiot? My five-year-old granddaughter can carry out your tasks without thinking. Please, don't push me today, Maribel."

"If you didn't want to be bothered, you should have stayed home."

The blood drained from Rachel's face.

"Uuuuh First Lady, I wasn't expecting you. I thought you were Maribel."

"Hhmmm, we've all been fooled about who each other is supposed to be. I'm not here for conversation. I just wanted to tell you to have your things out of this office by the end of the day."

"Is that Pastor's decision?"

Helen's eyes bulged. She thought to leap across the desk and grab Rachel by the throat. Instead, she stared directly into her eyes with a scowl, "You don't have a Pastor anymore. You crossed that line. Now, by the end of the day, you'd better be OUT of this church!"

"Or what? Are you threatening me?" Rachel's words bounced off of Helen's back as the door slammed behind her.

12

Have you ever needed someone, a shoulder just to cry on, to ease the agony, and find tranquility? Ooooh just have a sweet and gentle touch, that speaks of words of love that mean so much. Ordinary just won't do, I need someone my Lord I need someone. That someone is you. That someone is you. I don't need and ordinary, I don't need an ordinary Love, Lord I need your gentle touch.

The smooth, harmonious melodies mingling with the thoughts lodged in Helen's heart caused her to stop in her tracks.

"Oh God, I need you. I don't know who I am anymore. I feel like my very existence is being extinguished. What am I supposed to do?" She gazed at the bottle of prescribed sleeping pills in her hand. "I just want to sleep. No.....I want to die. I really want to die. I've lost everything. The words of the song continued interceding on her behalf as tears began to flow.

So many weaknesses and faults, I've got to learn to share the inner most and secret thoughts.

"God," she whispered, "I don't deserve this."

The song continued, *Lord I need a special touch, it would mean so very much. Close friends, they don't seem to understand. Problems in your life, so complex you say who can comprehend. Tragedy when you need relief, only Jesus Christ can supply your need, sweet and gentle touch that will speak a word of Love that means so much.*

Holding the pills in her hands, Helen sat on the floor rocking back and forth wailing so hard that her face began to swell. As the wailing turned to sobs, then sniffles Helen said, "Lord, I don't know what to do. I ache deep down past my soul. Now face down on the floor, she continued, "If you don't help me now, I'm not going to make it." Still sobbing, "Help me, please, please, please Lord, help me!"

She hadn't noticed Payton crack the door. His stomach in knots over the agony he now witnessed executed by his choices.

The song continued, *it's not an ordinary love, a Love that would die for me, stretch out his arms, yeah, yeah. It's not an ordinary love.*

Without contemplating Helen's response, Payton knelt down beside her, lifted her upright and wrapped her in his arms. They wept bitterly. Helen could not pull herself away from his chest. The more they cried the more she melted. Payton removed the bottle from her hands and kissed them. Holding her face in his hands, he kissed her swollen, tear stained eyes.

"I'm sorry, baby. I'm so, so sorry. I wish I could make this all go away. What I've done is inexcusable, but I can't live without you."

Helen couldn't respond, her heart still pleading "God help me." Knowing fully that her emotions were shipwrecked, she never uttered a word. A part of her wanted to beg Payton to stop what he was doing and save their marriage. A part of her would do anything to make things right again. *What if he didn't want to stop,* she thought. Helen tried to formulate a sentence but no words could escape through the mangled, twisted agony lodged in her throat. Her pleading eyes asked, "Do you love her?"

Payton sat hesitant and uncertain in her quietness. She was always outspoken and opinionated, feisty. He looked into her eyes without ever hearing her thoughts, "I have only loved you, Helen. I know it sounds crazy but it's the truth. I love you and only you. Please, think about forgiving me."

Helen looked into his eyes still unable to respond. Knowing that her fight lay dormant for now, Payton hugged her tight and whispered, "I miss you," through soft whispery kisses along her neck. "I miss you so much. I miss us."

13

Helen sat at the kitchen table sipping a cup of tea trying to gather her thoughts in an effort to plan out the day. Payton walked into the room.

"How are you this morning?"

Helen responded softly. "I'm not sure…I'm here. I'd like to talk to you before you leave."

Payton pulled out a chair wanting to talk as well with no idea where to begin. He felt as though he just stepped onto the platform of a guillotine. Attempting to touch her hand, Helen's reflexes caused her to withdraw quickly.

"Let's just talk," she said. "I have some questions that I need to be answered."

Payton withdrew his hand and swallowed hard. Regardless of past circumstances, they always stayed connected. This was the first time Payton ever felt real separation from his *Peach*, as he affectionately called her at times. He could not bear the distance between them.

Helen played with her fingers, "I've thought about this situation extensively. It plagues me in my sleep and assaults me during the day. My words may not come out exactly right, so just listen." Her tone turned cool and low. "This is an atrocity and I don't even know how to begin to deal with it. We have created so much together. We have generations, a daughter and granddaughter, a ministry and pages, upon pages of history. I'm afraid to imagine what has been conceived from what you've done. Every time you," she hesitated as she tried to compose herself, but the tears won out, "lay with this woman, you created seeds.

"It's like you deliberately took a jack hammer, cracked our foundation and dropped seeds of selfishness, immorality, and abomination between the cracks. Now everyone that's intertwined with our lives will reap weeds of destruction, disaster, desolation, and only God knows what else."

The words stung Payton like a swarm of a thousand bees. He thought to himself, *where did she get these analogies?* Helen always had an uncanny knack for painting vivid imagery with words. *So aggravating*, he reflected.

Helen broke his thoughts, "how many Payton?"

"What!" He said almost stumbling over those three words.

"Did I stutter? How many women? I want to think it's just one, but my heart and my senses won't allow me to rest with that thought."

He turned away unsure of how to answer. *What did she really know? Did she see me prior to last Thursday night?* "Helen please," he spoke carefully.

"If you can't begin by being honest, then we really don't have anything to preserve," she scoffed as she began to push her chair away from the table.

"Okay, okay," he said swallowing hard again. She pulled her seat back to the table and waited for his response with piercing eyes. "All I can say is it's been more than one person, but I don't think we should do this."

"Mmmm, don't do this? Please don't tell me what we should or should not do. How many is more than one? Five, ten, fifteen?"

"Helen, what does it matter, how many?"

"It matters," she spat. "And why are you saying more than one person? Are we talking men and women?"

"Now you're being ridiculous," Payton grumbled as agitation began to break through the tone of his voice.

"No, it's not ridiculous," Helen returned. "I would have never thought we would darken a damnable place like this, but here we are. I need to know who and what I'm dealing with." Tapping the table with her fingers, Helen waited. "Okay, you don't want to answer? Here's an easier question. Whose house was that?" Payton sat unresponsively.

After a few moments, Payton responded, "I think answers would add more pain to the situation."

Helen fired back, "The least you could do is be a man about it and own up to the truth. Whose house was it!!!?" Her scalding words burned with intensity.

"I'm not going to sit here and allow you to interrogate me." Payton tried to remain calm as he pushed his chair from the table.

"Fine, have it your way. I thought it better if I heard it from you. It will come out. But until you're ready to come clean about everything, we have nothing." Payton knew she was right, but he couldn't bring himself to divulge the flagrant truth. "By the way, so you're not surprised," Helen snapped, "Rachel is finished. I terminated her."

Payton's pride began to swell. "This situation does not give you the power to stomp around and make irrational decisions. You should have come to me first."

Helen stood with a look of disdain in her eyes. "You had sex with this woman. No, I'll take it a step further. You had, rather is having a relationship with this woman. Only God knows how long this has been going on. I know you don't think that you can be a Pastor to her? And what about her husband, your Assistant Pastor? What will you say to him? How do you plan to deal with Ray, Payton?"

"Helen, you are not the overseer of the church! Don't go over my head making decisions about my church members or staff!"

"Your church!?"

"Helen, you know what I mean. Just talk to me first."

Helen laughed contemptuously, "Talk! Did you say talk to you first? I think you're on some new type of drug. I don't have to talk to you about anything. Did you talk to me first?"

"Look, Helen," Payton growled, "I admit, I messed up. But guess what, this sumptuous lifestyle that you're accustomed to, I provide that. You buy what you want, wear what you want and drive whatever you want. Don't think for a moment that you're going to hold me hostage. If you think you can do better, go ahead, I dare you. I said I was sorry, I never meant it to happen. But don't threaten me. The twenty questions are going to stop. You really don't want the answers. You can't handle the answers."

Panic began to sit in the pit of Helen's stomach but her pride would not allow her to lose control. She shifted back into a cool low tone. "Wow, you have the audacity to say that....to me. You really think you did all of this by yourself? You are an arrogant....who do you think you are? Did someone bewitch you? What happened to you?"

Payton roared, "What happened to you? Maybe that's the question you need to ask yourself. Maybe if you traveled with me like I asked, none of this would have ever happened."

"Don't you dare try to push this off on your needs not being met! I'm with you every available chance." Helen paused abruptly, "You know what Payton, it does not matter. Have a nice life."

"Have a nice life? Where will you go, Helen? You have too much pride to say anything to anyone and you're too persnickety to stay anywhere. Sell that to someone who's buying." Payton continued in a gruff tone, "And yes, it matters. You know it and I know it. You really think you're perfect, don't you? Think you got the upper hand here. If you as much as breathe another command to anyone at my church...." Payton, acutely aware of his loss of control headed for the front door without completing his thought. "I don't have to threaten you, Helen. I'm telling you straight, don't do it again!"

Helen's response crashed against the wooden front door.

14

Ray Morgan sunk down in the tufted leather sofa in the living room of the carriage house looking around in bewilderment. The complications surrounding the ministry began to coagulate into menacing shapes looming overhead. Although his silent observance caused great conflict within his spirit, he could not bring himself to confront Payton about his impetuous behavior.

*Who am I to judge, h*e thought to himself. *We're men just like everyone else, prone to the same passions and struggles.* Raymond saw the change in Payton, never the less his support was unfailing. The shift was extremely subtle; he couldn't pinpoint the origin. The elusive poison released from their selfish decisions quickly attacked the senses leaving the congregation in a crazed, self-gratifying state. Some were spiritually deaf, others blind, but more awful than these, confusion and irrationality spread about in epidemic proportions.

Ray released a low groan as he rubbed his temples. The slamming of a car door aroused him from the oppressive thoughts. "It's about time. Good God from Zion, you're forty-five minutes late," Ray spouted as he opened the front door. "I have a good mind to…. I'm sorry; I thought you were the cleaning crew."

"Raymond, what are you doing here? Is this one of your houses? Do you know what's …uhm, never mind, I have to go."

"First Lady, wait a minute. What just happened? How did she find out about this house?" Perplexed, he pulled out his phone and punched in Helen's number. "First Lady, this is Raymond, please call me back. Obviously, you're shaken. I'm not sure what's going on but….just call me back."

Raymond slapped his phone shut. A thin line of realization seeped through his mind, and he made a mental note to pay attention to his wife's whereabouts. For a split second he thought, *where did that come from*? Fear began to pierce a small hole through his being. Ray took a deep gulp and whispered through clenched teeth, "We are being exposed. Lord, have mercy on us."

15

"I've got to get out of here," Helen muttered under her breath. "So you're the man huh? Okay, Mr. Man, you got this! You want to play? I'll play it your way. Since you're so lonely and needy, let's see how your little girlfriends fix you up this go round."

The knock on the door interrupted her tirade, "Great! Just great! Who is it?"

Helen opened the door and before she could say a word Lydia grabbed her in a tight embrace and whispered in her ear, "God knows, Helen. It matters to Him about you." Lydia's embrace was so full of peace; Helen began to break again.

Through intermittent sniffles, Helen asked, "He knows what Lydia? And what are you doing here? I told you that everything was fine."

"I know you did, several times but I just needed to see you. Something has changed since our last conversation." Lydia paused waiting for Helen to fill in the blanks. "Helen, what happened? I went to the church looking for you and one of the young ladies said I might find you at home. Helen, talk to me!"

"Lydia, I'm horrible as I'm sure you can see. So, what does God know?" Does He know that I feel like I'm dying? Does He know that I actually want to die today? Exactly what does He know?"

The quiet blanketed the room. "Helen," Lydia said softly, "He knows what has been happening in your church and with your husband. He showed me your tears and allowed me to feel your anguish and torment. You must trust and depend on Him."

"Trust and depend? I have done that and look at my life, Lydia. My husband hasn't had one affair, only God knows how many. For twenty-seven years I've been faithful to him and God." Sobbing through patchy breaths, "I've fasted and prayed for Payton to have boldness in speech and Favor in the community. I've fasted and prayed for the ministry to thrive and reproduce good fruit, for lives to be changed and people to be delivered. I trusted that God would keep us, Lyd. I can't do it anymore."

"Helen, I've only had a glimpse of what's happening. You have a right to be angry but please don't stop believing now."

"You know what, Lyd, I am so over God and the church. I'm done. Payton can have it all."

With a look of concession, Lydia dropped her head and wept openly. "My heart is so broken for you, Helen."

Lydia's sincerity softened Helen's demeanor for a moment. "You're a good friend Lydia. Just pray for me."

"I am praying for you. Do you mind if we pray before I leave?"

Helen's eyes rolled, "I didn't mean now."

Lydia grabbed her hands. "Now is as good a time as any."

16

Helen jumped from the frying pan into the fire. Aunt Pauline, affectionately known as Auntie, was not one to reckon with. As badly as Helen wanted to conceal her internal injuries, she knew Auntie could sense something by her "I've been waiting to hear from you child. When are you coming down?"

Helen almost wanted to respond by telling Auntie she wasn't coming down, but she could not muster the strength to pull off a believable lie. She told Auntie that she would arrive later in the evening.

Arriving in Peace Lake, Florida eased a bit of the tension knotted in Helen's stomach. The drive from the airport would buy her just enough time to make herself presentable, and make a few phone calls.

"Hi Nesy, this is Mom. I just wanted to hear my baby girl's voice. How is she doing? I hope you and Stefon are doing well. Let the baby call me later. By the way, I'm out of town for a little bit checking in on Auntie. Look to talk to you soon."

It was well past lunch and the last few days of meager meals began to echo through Helen's stomach. "I hear you, I hear you," Helen said as she pulled off of the highway. The sky was remarkably blue; the air was crisp and clear. With outstretched arms, face high towards the sky, and back arched, Helen inhaled as much of the sun sea concoction as she could before slowly releasing it with fragments of her grim morning.

"I could get used to this." Helen smiled shielding her eyes from the direct sunlight glancing across the bay. The quaint upscale bistro called Jacque's nestled between two medium rise hotels with a spectacular bay view welcomed passersby with aromas of freshly baked bread.

A bronze toned, model type, Mexican man greeted Helen. "Good afternoon madam. How many?"

"Just one," Helen replied following the host to a small square table for two.

"Such a beautiful lady dining alone? Pity."

"It's quite fine. I actually prefer it, thank you." Helen knew the clear, crisp air that she allowed to overpower every crevice in her mind would soon wear off, but she wasn't ready to surrender to this morning's reverberating shouting match. Subconsciously wincing from the thought of the sharp words, she was startled by a waiter sitting a glass of wine in front of her.

"Compliments of the gentlemen at the back table, Madam."

"Excuse me? Kindly return that to whoever sent it, thank you."

"Yes, Madam," the waiter replied.

Helen muttered, "He must be out of his mind. He doesn't want to cross this bridge. The audacity to think......."

"I see we're talking to ourselves these days."

Helen's head whipped around, "Excuse me? Oh my goodness," she smiled as she stood to hug a long time friend. "I know you did not send me a drink? Have you lost your mind?"

"Not since I last checked. I just wanted to ruffle your feathers a little bit seeing that you were always the church going type."

"True, true," Helen laughed, "And you never were."

"You know Paul told Timothy to drink a little wine for the stomach's sake. Am I right?"

Helen smirked, "Still trying to find a glitch in the book to suit your own appetites, aren't you?"

"You know Len, some things never change."

Helen giggled on the inside at the sound of the childhood nickname she had not heard in years. She could hardly believe she was staring into the face of her childhood best friend, Victor Lawson. Helen, affectionately known as Len to Victor, met him when she was seven years old. They spent every summer together until college.

Victor lived down the road from Auntie and Uncle David. Before Uncle David went home to be with the Lord, Victor would ride his bike up the road at the crack of dawn only to be chided by Uncle David for interrupting his breakfast. After the ten minute talking to, Victor would end up at the breakfast table like one of the family members, talking sports.

"Len, you haven't changed one bit."

Helen blushed. "Well, I can't say the same about you. You look totally different."

"Thank you, I think," Victor responded sheepishly. Should I still look like the scrawny, four eyed boy that hung out with the preacher's daughter for divine protection?"

"Stop it, you did not," Helen quipped.

"You're right. Maybe because... well, I had my reasons."

"How are you?" Helen sang.

"I'm well. I would be even better if you would allow me to join you? I was just about to order when I saw you come in."

"Oh, please do," Helen continued melodically. "What are you doing here?"

"I'm here on business. I don't have to ask what you're doing here. How is your Auntie?"

"She is doing as well as can be expected. I'm just checking in on her to make sure she's behaving. She still thinks she's as young as I am. This is unbelievable! I would not have expected to see you here in a million years."

"Yeah, crazy isn't it. So Len, how has life been treating you? You look Exquisite. Not that you ever looked badly. Girl, you haven't changed at all. You still look like you're in your twenties."

Victor studied Helen's beauty raising his eyebrows in admiration. She hadn't changed much. Still refined, slender, and as graceful as ever. He remembered that Helen always peered at the world with a direct gaze through almond shaped, dark brown eyes beneath manicured brows."

"Okay, hold on. Are you trying to get me to buy?"

Laughing out loud, Victor replied, "No I'm okay in that area. As a matter of fact, this is on me. I needed a little sunshine in my life today and here you are."

"Yeah, okay. The magnificent rays of the sun in all its glory and splendor proclaiming the entire day isn't enough?" Helen chuckled lightly.

"Still the same Len, aren't you?"

"Always," she snickered.

"So fill me in, Len. What's new?"

"Life is life. I'm just living it."

"Oh, that's different coming from you, the cheerleader of life."

Fumbling through her pocket book, Helen pulled out her wallet. "This is my joy right here."

"She is adorable. Victor studied the photo. "She has her grandmother's smile."

"Yes, she does. I love her desperately."

"You know; you look too young to be called grand mom?"

"My name is not grand mom, it's MeeMee."

"Oh, okay. I guess you can pass for a MeeMee."

"What about you, Victor. Any grandchildren yet?"

"My son is barely grown. He's not ready yet. Bedsides, I'm not looking forward to any grand babies for quite a while."

"You mean, you're not ready yet," Helen smirked. "So what kind of business are you about in this neck of the woods."

"I'm here representing a number of investment firms that need to close a few deals over the next week." Victor was in his mid-forties, six feet three, gray brown eyes, and sandy brown, curly hair cut short and tapered on the sides.

Helen raised her eyebrows. "That makes sense."

"What?" Victor responded with a sheepish look on his face.

"The look of success. The ice draped around your arm and fingers. You look like you just waltzed out of the 'Top 10 Most Successful Men' featured in Black Enterprise Magazine."

Prosperity made Victor look confident, sleek, and alluring. His well-defined physique bulged beneath the tailor-made, silk, beige and blue window pane blazer, and navy pants. It was always Victor's fine hair, wanting eyes, and boyish banter that allowed his rites of passage with women that otherwise would not have been introduced to him.

"I haven't done too badly for myself." Victor smiled moving his arm from the table, placing it on his lap. "I guess I over indulge a little in the finer things in life."

"Oh please Victor, for as long as I've known you, you've over indulged. You were always driven by your insatiable appetite for the more expensive things in life. Your watch is beautiful. Let me see."

"Oh sure, Len, be candid why don't you." He extended his arm across the table.

"This has to be every bit five thousand dollars."

"Close," he uttered.

"This is a Euro Geneve, isn't it?"

"Yes," he responded with raised eyebrows. "You know your watches."

"Not really. I happened to look at one for my husband not long ago. Whatever it costs Victor, it's gorgeous. If you have the means, enjoy it. Life is too short."

"I knew the "Rah-Rah" girl couldn't hide out for long."

Helen beckoned the waiter to bring the check. "Yeah well, the "Rah-Rah" girl had better be going. I've let time get away from me."

"Stop that," Victor fussed. "I told you, this is on me."

"Okay, I'm not going to fight you Daddy Warbucks."

"Thank you. It's not very often that I get to dine with such an exquisite woman that's not after me for my money."

"That's sad to hear." Helen frowned, "somehow, I think you enjoy playing the game."

Victor smiled, "A little bit."

Helen made a scowling face.

"Okay, okay, I confess. I like the game."

"That's better. Be yourself, Victor." Helen hugged Victor around the neck. "Thank you again. It was so great to see you."

"Len, how long will you be in town? Maybe we can meet and catch up on life and talk about old times?"

"Mmmmm, I'm not sure, and I doubt if I'll have time to do anything."

"Here, take my card and promise you'll call if you get time. I'm here until the middle of next week."

"Okay," Helen smiled, "If I get some free time."

17

Payton sat in the League of Pastor's meeting, his
Blackberry emitting an annoying vibration every few
minutes. The pending City Wide Revival was the topic
of discussion. Pastor Little of the Baptist Church
chimed into the cacophony demanding that they all act
on equal terms. "There needs to be some type of
continuity. If I close my church down Sunday morning,
why shouldn't all of us for the sake of the souls that we
are trying to win."

Pastor Allen of the Full Gospel Church barked, "My
Sunday morning service is my strongest offertory
service and I'm not willing to shut that service down."
Many nods affirmed his position.

Pastor Blackburn from the Methodist Church could
not sit silent any longer. "Gentlemen, what we're
looking to produce from this revival will cost us. Have
we veered so far off course that we've forgotten that we
can't offer God something that cost us nothing? The
Sunday morning culmination of this revival is going to
bring in a harvest of souls that this city has never seen.

An offering can't compare. Besides, where is your faith? We instruct our parishioners to trust God. What are we doing?"

Pastor Shepherd retorted, "Say whatever you want, people are not going to pay their tithe and offering in the absence of a service so…what you're proposing won't work for me."

Payton finally interjected, "There's no need to continue deliberating over this issue. Let's reconvene Friday, 10 a.m., my church. I strongly suggest that we all pray about this matter so that we come ready to finalize all of the revival plans on that day. Is everyone in agreement?" Nods, grunts, and mumbles confirmed. "Great gentlemen, be blessed."

18

Payton walked into a web of confusion.

"Good afternoon Pastor. I don't know if you want to be here right now, but… "

"But what? What's going on?" Payton raised his eyebrows.

Maribel continued in a whisper, "Well, First Lady was here yesterday and from the looks of things Minister Morgan is….."

Rachel finished her sentence, "Going to find a new secretary."

"Okay Mommie, but I'm not a secretary. I'm an assistant," Maribel smirked.

Without acknowledging the ensuing cat fight, Payton walked away and closed the door to his office. Before it was fully closed, a hand pushed through the small crack.

"You can't keep avoiding me," Rachel railed.

"What do you want, Rachel."

"I want to know how your wife had the authority to come here and tell me I'd better leave the church. Didn't you get my messages? Are you firing me?"

"Rachel, right now I don't know what I'm doing."

"You're the Pastor and supposed to be the man, what do you mean you don't know?"

Rachel's statement of ignition set off a cannonball reaction. Payton's fist pounded into the desk as he bellowed, "You crossed the line. Get out of my office!"

Rachel knew not to respond. She'd never seen this type of fury in her Pastor. As she quickly walked out she thought, *this is far from over.*

Finally quiet, Payton leaned back in the heavy leather chair. "Aaaah, this feels good." As he drank in the League of Pastors meeting and his fight with Helen, Payton grew intoxicated with exhaustion. He studied a picture of himself and Helen laying face to face on a beach towel gazing into each other's eyes. He could remember their exact conversation and the plans they were making to cap the perfect day. Immediately to the right, another picture of Helen glared at him mockingly. Payton dropped his head into his hands wondering if they would ever recover.

Maribel barged through Payton's office door, tripping over a chair, pouncing on the TV remote. "O my God, O my God," she screamed hysterically. "O my God Pastor. Look at this."

The large flat screen TV came to life, "Breaking news! Approximately one hour ago, a young woman was seen throwing herself 200 feet off the Key Bridge. Reports confirm that she drove her car in lane one, center span of the Bridge, climbed over the guardrail and jumped. Her identification is being withheld pending notification of the family. There is no further information, but we will keep you updated. You heard it here first on News Now."

Payton sat frozen to his chair. The cameras flashed a picture of the car with its personalized license plate in full view. He could not utter a word. Maribel cried hysterically, ranting back in forth in English and Spanish. "O my God, that's, that's," she could not get the name out of her mouth.

Payton interrupted, "don't jump to conclusions."

"Her license plate, her, lic…"

"I know Maribel. I see it, but let's get a conclusive report from family or the police. Go splash some water on your face and try to calm down. Where is everyone?" He whispered under his breath.

Rachel ran in, "what's going on?"

Payton motioned for Rachel to take Maribel out of the office. "What's happening?" Rachel barked, but Payton's look stopped her before she could form another sentence.

"Get her out of here," Payton growled.

19

Nina sat in her living room gazing at the Anchor person as they showed live feeds of the suicide site.

"Approximately two hours ago, a young woman, mid-twenties stopped her 2005 Ford Five Hundred in lane one, center span of the Key Bridge, climbed over the guardrail, and jumped 200 feet into the murky river. Passing motorists jammed the police station with calls reporting a subject falling off the bridge. Rescue crews responded immediately to the scene and the police buoy system was used to recover the victim's body just a few minutes ago. Just in, the victim's name is Tara Rubenstein. Shown here in a recent photo with her 14month old daughter, she seemingly had everything to live for. Let's talk to Sue, live outside of the victim's home."

"Yes Deborah, the mood is very dismal. The family is distraught with grief."

Ringing her hands and shaking on the inside, Nina spat at the TV, "Dag girl, I knew you were weak, but not like that. Okay Nina, think, think, think." Pacing back and forth in front of a tattered leopard sofa, she opened her cell phone frantically punching numbers several times before getting them right. Before the person on the other end could say hello Nina yelled, "Turn on the news. Turn on the freakin news now! Do you see this? WE KILLED HER!!!" After a few moments of silence listening to the voice on the other end of the phone, the line went dead.

Nina plopped onto the sofa that bottomed out under her thick mass because of broken springs. Stout with a short tapered haircut, round face and barely there thin lips, Nina rolled onto her side and laid in the fetal position. She closed her eyes tight, recalling the first time she met Tara during her second visit to the morning worship service at Spirit and Truth.

Nina smirked at her outlandish dress that day. She wore camo Army pants with a black tank top displaying her tattoos. On her right arm 'jus da 2 of us' and on the other arm up and down the length of her arm 'my tears your fears'. Although she loved her body art, most of the time she displayed it for kicks and giggles anticipating the faces and reactions of the self-righteous. She always wondered who they thought they were to judge her. But, not Tara, she walked over and greeted Nina warmly. The piercings, tattoos, and army fatigues didn't faze her one bit. Tara was a little naive but genuinely nice.

"Tara," Nina whimpered, "I'm sorry, I'm so, so sorry. It wasn't supposed to be like this. I admit, what we did was cruel and thoughtless, but never in my wildest dreams did I,….we, think you'd do something like this."

Nina picked up the remote, her hands barely able to control it, clicked and the screen faded to black. "Okay, okay, I know what you need," talking to herself. She stumbled to the kitchen cabinet. "There you are Henne, you'll knock these jitters right out. Come on baby, work your magic." She gulped from the bottle of Hennessey and slammed it on the counter, exhaled and lit a black and mild.

Looking at the bottle quizzically, Nina asked, "Do you think this is our fault?" She puffed and gulped. "Yup, it is. You're right! Tara was sweet, innocent, and naïve. It was so easy. She never saw it coming." Several long gulps, "This is some serious stuff." A long drag, hands flailing in the air, "Why would you do that Tara? What was wrong with you that you'd pull some whacked out stuff like that? Crazy?!! That's it! Maybe you had a history of mental illness in your family. Yo, you know what? That sounds right doesn't it?"

Looking at the bottle, Nina took another swig, another drag. "I'm convinced there was something wrong with you Tara and I'm not taking the heavy for it."

20

Pauline Bell, also known as Auntie, was a petite woman of presence and stature with a soft, peculiar voice that emitted great strength. A widow for many years, she spent most of her time talking to the Lord and meditating on His Word. Many leaders and their wives flocked to Auntie's for prayer and counsel. Her house was known as the *House of Refuge* because of the great peace, the demonstration of love, and the Power of God through answered prayer. Auntie understood all too well that the greatest attack was on leadership in every area of life. She always said *there is something about the suffering and attacks on ministers and their families. If the enemy can create an open door for himself through the leader, he would have free reign over all that the leader possesses and consequently breed chaos, confusion and ultimately death.* Auntie also said on so many occasions, *often we have preachers and leaders, silly men and women who want something or someone more than they want God. They're drawn away by their own lust and erect their own idols in their hearts quickly lending the enemy their expertise in their own demise. You have to want all of God, He'll take nothing less.*

Auntie sat near the window in her rocker as the evening sun slowly slipped beyond the canopy of trees draped across the back yard. The day had been hot and spicy causing all the aromas of nature to collide into a pungent fragrance. Pauline was thrilled to detect a single, thread of sweet lavender in the biting odor.

Pulling out the ingredients for her famous cinnamon buns with cream cheese icing, Pauline recalled the times when that was all she had to do to make her little girl feel better.

"Lord, it's going to take more than cinnamon buns this go round. My girl's soul is in turmoil. Lord, give me the words, fill this place with your peace as you always do for those seeking refuge. Thank you for being who you are, the Almighty." Stopping in her tracks, she looked up and blew a kiss. "God, I love you. Now, how do I communicate to my baby that this is for her making? It's so easy to offend young people nowadays, especially when their hurting. Thank you for using me in another birthing process."

As the final rays of the sun disappeared, Pauline began to hum the song that rang in her soul all week. *The blood that Jesus shed for me, way back on Calvary, the blood that gives you strength, from day to day, it will never lose its power. It soothes my doubts and calms my fears and it dries my tears. The blood that gives me strength from day to day, it will never lose its power. It reaches to the highest mountain. It flows to the lowest valley. The blood that gives you strength from day to day, it will never lose its power.*

Auntie was so grateful that the young Elder from the church had come to serve her communion. The days of making it out to Sunday morning service consistently was long past. However, ministry was still alive and well in the comfort of her living room.

"Lord if these walls could talk." She giggled girlishly. "We've had some times in this house; the spiritual births, the miscarriages, and the many miracles I was privileged to see. One day I'll have to get my journals published and maybe all of my girls can benefit. We overcome by the blood of the lamb and the word of our testimonies."

21

The church's foyer was aligned with glass vases full of floral splendor set upon ornate cherry pedestals and window sills. The serene and refined simplicity of the stargazer lilies with a single splash of pink bursting from the middle offered peace and tranquility to the congregants walking in with fragmented bits of information bearing on broken hearts and confused minds.

The soft, tantalizing fragrance that permeated the atmosphere began to wilt under the oppressive moans of astonished friends and associates attempting to piece together different segments of information gathered from the news.

Questions flew back and forth. "Has anyone spoken with her family? Did they detect any signs of suicide? You know there are classic signs? Who pays attention to that sort of thing?"

Chandra, one of Tara's good friends uttered under her breath "I wish everyone would just shut up!" Sitting near the back of the church under a stained glass window of Jesus hanging on the cross with his head dangling to one side, Chandra glanced up and retorted, "How could this be allowed to happen?"

Mother Corbett slid next to Chandra almost unnoticed by her, stretched her arm the length of the pew behind Chandra's neck and whispered words of comfort in her ear. As the tears blazing down her face stung her cheeks, Chandra promised herself she'd find out why.

Payton stood at the pulpit silently until the soft drone was replaced by an intense hush. "Brothers and sisters it is with great grief and horrific astonishment that we've learned that one of our own, Sister Tara Rubenstein, took her life today."

Silence then gasps mixed with sniffles and muffled cries. "We are not clear about many things as of yet. I, along with a small contingency of clergy, will meet with Tara's family immediately after this meeting. I do have one request. Because of the sensitive nature surrounding Tara's death, please do not respond to gestures from the press for your comments. We have designated clergy personnel that will gladly speak on behalf of the entire church body. As individuals, we do not want to bring any shame or embarrassment to the family or the church with off colored statements. The mothers will be organizing the efforts towards the families' needs. Your cooperation and prayers are greatly appreciated. If any of you would like to speak with clergy or counselors regarding this tragic event, please meet Pastor Morgan in the chapel immediately after this meeting."

Chandra sat expressionlessly. "That's it? Embarrassment! Shame! Does it matter why she did this?" She screamed on the inside, but no words escaped.

22

Helen drove down the quiet back road and subconsciously checked her lipstick and hair. *What am I doing* she thought as she focused her eyes back on the road. *No one out here cares how I look.*

Darkness began its invasion as the sun slipped behind the horizon and the stifling heat and haunting images began to swirl around Helen's forehead. How many women had she counselled, cried and prayed with? How many times had she said to them, we have to trust God with our emotions? "I don't want to trust you to fix it, God. It shouldn't be," she murmured. "This just should not be!"

The tightened muscles in Helen's stomach compelled her to exhale allowing a low groan to escape filling the car with weariness and reminding her that she barely touched her dinner.

The very sight of the small rancher with light filtering from every window cajoled a smile. She loved how Auntie turned on every light in the house to greet her. Tilting her head to the side, eyes full of uncertainty and questions, Helen wished this was one of her summer visits of old. She remembered flying down to Auntie's every summer hanging out at the beach and riding bikes with Victor. No cares, no worries, just the occasional revival, and mandatory bible study. At Auntie's house, Helen experienced her first spiritual awakening and grasped biblical insight into many Old Testament stories.

Helen scowled, "what was it all for?" She walked in the door, dropped her bags, walked over to the frail little woman, put her head in Auntie's lap and wept. The weeping turned to whimpering as Auntie's soothing words saturated Helen's soul. Auntie whispered over and over again as she softly stroked Helen's head pulling her hair away from her face. "Thank you Lord for peace, we're so grateful for your peace. Every emotion must come into subjection to your peace."
Helen could feel the peace of God washing over her soul as all she wanted to do was sleep. Auntie continued to stroke her head, "Things will look better in the morning, baby."

23

Helen tossed and turned, looking at the bedside clock for the tenth time before finally getting out of the bed. Standing at the window with her arms crossed over her chest as if guarding her heart, peering into the dark, she never felt so alone. The bitterness and pain that pierced her soul were unexplainable.

"Lord, why would you allow Payton to do this? I don't understand! You could have stopped him. You stopped Balaam in his tracks with a talking donkey. You allowed Jonah to be thrown overboard and swallowed by a fish for disobeying you. You even struck Paul off of his horse and blinded him to get his attention. Why not stop Payton?"

Anxiety began to blanket the room. Helen could hardly breathe as her face broke out in a cold sweat. She grabbed her heart and sat on the edge of the bed. "I don't know what I'm dealing with Lord but I know it's more than I'm willing to face." Rocking back and forth, she mumbled, "I can't, I can't, Oh God, I can't. This is so unfair," Helen whined. I'm tired of doing the right thing. I don't want to forgive. Why couldn't he do the right thing? He's the chosen one. I just want to… I just want… I don't know what I want."

Helen felt disconnected from everyone and everything. Insecurity ravaged any speck of confidence daring to represent any good over the past twenty-seven years. Every past triumph, all of their successes seemed to buckle under the weight of this oppression.

"Lord, I just want to feel safe. I want to feel loved. I need to feel like I matter."

Helen thought about the church members, especially the church mothers. They loved her greatly and she loved them right back. Mother Corbett had become somewhat of a surrogate mother to Helen always keeping a watchful eye for any and everything.

How would she walk out of their lives? What would they think of her leaving? Would they accept a new First Lady? She cringed to think of the many barracudas that would vie for that position.

Helen shrugged her shoulders, "be my guest," she grumbled. "He'll be advertising for a new one soon. I've played second to the ministry long enough. I've shared our time, our home and you Payton, on so many different levels, but I will not share our intimacy. I did not sign up for this! Keep the house, the car and anything else that you feel I'm so attached too.

"Those things never defined me as a woman. They are just things. I can always get things. What about our family you idiot? We had something special." She thought for a moment. "Maybe I was wrong. I thought we had something special. I thought we had a genuine type of love. How did I fool myself for so long?"

Helen's heart began pounding against her chest. "All I ever wanted was YOU! How stupid could you be Payton?"

A tiny light sliced through the darkness blinking constantly. The light drew Helen into a hypnotic gaze. After a few moments, she shook herself. "I don't want to talk. Leave me alone!"

The searing ache that drowned every organ in Helen's body caused her to moan and groan. Finally, Helen stretched herself toward the dresser to grab the phone. There were twenty-two missed calls. She tapped the text messaging application, fifteen text messages. Scrolling through the numbers, Nesy, Nesy, Nesy, Payton, Payton, Michelle, Lydia and a few others.

Helen stopped scrolling at an unfamiliar number. She tapped the screen to open the message and her heart fluttered as she read, *'your husband is a lucky man. After all of these years, you still got it! Dinner…delicious. Seeing you…Heaven. Vic.'*

Before Helen realized, she responded. *'How did you get my number?'* Send.

'A good investigator never reveals his source. So glad you're up. Can't stop thinking about you.' Helen froze. After ten minutes of no response, her phone vibrated. She stared at the number, sucked in her stomach and answered with a whisper. "Victor!"

He cut her off, "I'm not trying to disrespect you, Len. I apologize. You know me. It's just…seeing you made me homesick."

"It's okay Victor. I guess I forgive you for stalking me." They laughed and exchanged friendly banter for a few minutes before ending the call.

Helen contemplated seeing Victor again. Her heart raced. If for no other reason, she loved the way he made over her with his back ended comments. She wondered what would happen if she just went along with one of his comments. How would it play out? She never fed into anything Victor said. Sure, he was handsome enough, but he was Victor, the boy next store. Helen blushed, flooded with memories of a younger Victor stroking her bangs from her eyes, and wiping the dirt from her hands after they'd fallen riding bikes.

Victor's eyes glistened whenever they talked. Helen gasped, "Even tonight, his eyes glistened." She shook her head and spoke evenly to herself. "Helen get a hold of yourself. You do not need this kind of problem. It won't solve anything." A quiet thought invaded her mind. *Payton deserves the same thing he gave you. You'll feel better.*

Helen was hooked. It was just the right thing to distract her attention and anesthetize her pain. She laid back down hugging the pillow tightly against her body, "Why not? I'm still young and desirable. Victor has always appreciated me. I just never gave him the chance. Maybe I should this time. Just don't cross the line, Helen," she reasoned.

"Twenty-seven years. I've never given thought to another man. What is wrong with me? Oh God, forgive me. This is not the answer." She quieted for a while. Tears welled in her eyes. Helen envisioned the rise of the garage door seeing her husband and Rachel embraced. "You know what Helen?" She spoke to herself defiantly. "Get the divorce! Payton chose this road. He started this! He made the choice for me. I want him to see how it feels to ache in parts of his body that he didn't know existed. I want him to feel betrayed and deserted."

A new battle raged slowly diminishing the minuscule amounts of Helen's will to salvage what was left of her marriage. She looked forward to the chase from Victor. She knew he would only go as far as she would allow. She repeatedly played their conversation over in her mind. Helen opened the text message and read it several times contemplating Victor lying next to her stroking her hair, speaking softly.

A faint sound broke through the silence; first a low hum then a medium melody. *'Jesus knows all about our struggles, He will guide us til the day is done. There's not a friend like the lowly Jesus, no not one, no not one.'*

Auntie's delicate voice continued to seep beneath the door. Helen closed her phone, grabbed the pillow, holding it tight against her chest and stomach until she drifted off to sleep.

24

Helen finally emerged from her bedroom to the smell of fresh cinnamon buns.

"She lives! I hope you slept some." Auntie smiled, poured two cups of tea and served the buns. "I peeked in on you a few times to make sure you were still breathing." She chuckled, "It's been a few days." Auntie walked over to hug Helen. "Did you rest any?"

"Auntie, I don't know if I was asleep or awake. I can't shut my mind down."

"Yes, the mind is the battlefield child. It takes great discipline and restraint to get to the point of casting down imaginations and every high thing that exalts itself against the knowledge of the truth. You have to choose to bring into captivity every thought to the obedience of Christ. That encompasses our out of control emotions. This just may be your starting point. So tell me, child, what brought you to visit your old Auntie?"

Helen recalled the entire story. Auntie sighed. "First things first baby. You are in a lot of pain and somewhat confused but you have to snap out of it and do what's necessary. What is the Lord asking of you?"

"Nothing Auntie. How could He possibly ask me for something at a time like this?"

"Know your Father, child. His ways are not our ways and His thoughts totally different from ours. Baby, all parties involved are responsible for their choices and its God's business how He decides to chasten them, and He will. He is a righteous father and judge. He will allow everybody space and time for repentance. Either way, He will repay for the deeds done in this body."

Helen's heart was bent. "Well, God needs to crack Payton's back wide open. Auntie, he is such a…, a…jerk. He doesn't deserve God's mercy."

"Sugah, none of us do. Baby, he's just a man."

"I know Auntie. I guess I'm having trouble believing that Payton would betray me." Helen paused to compose herself before continuing in a broken voice. "We've shared a lot of years. Auntie, we are or were like….fine china….a cup and saucer. We fit, finishing each other's sentences and thoughts. We felt each other when things went wrong. We read each other's eyes and shared similar goals. And passion, that was off the chart. I don't know Auntie. Maybe I lack perception and just wanted to believe that, but it was good for quite a while. I mean, we struggled and worked at it like everybody else, but overall, I thought it was really good.

"I've never known Payton to be duplicitous. Either he's a master deceiver or I just totally missed it. He never seemed unhappy or unfulfilled. Oh! Maybe now I know why. You know what else? Maybe my mind is running rampant, but Auntie, I know there's more to this than meets the eye. My thoughts are jumbled, but I keep getting small glimpses of the past and somehow I know it all connects.

"I saw a HUD One form on Ray's desk a while ago. It caught my attention, but I shrugged it off as one of the church's projects. I am sure it documents that carriage house, which means Ray could know what's going on. But, that doesn't make sense, does it? And, at the last dinner meeting, Rachel ran her hand lightly across Payton's back in just a way that took it beyond good taste. How foolish have I been, Auntie?

"Listen, baby. Don't be so hard on yourself. Now that you know, you will have to get past yourself and deal with the real issue. Getting past yourself will be one of your greatest feats, but you can do it. Then you must accept that you cannot deal naturally with something that began in the spirit. I know you don't see it yet, but this is spiritual. There's a pulsing, raging, stronghold at the point of origin of this thing. It doesn't listen to reason, or to the law, or any set of morals. This spirit's primary desire is to cast Christ down from His Excellency through you, your husband, and the ministry. This spirit is calculating and will pick off one person at a time if need be. Do not try to reason with anyone involved. Don't depend on them doing what's right or following any laws. They are beyond that point. You must depend on the Word of God and focus, then re-focus, and re-focus again. The Lord will give you the right Word to speak and pray over this situation."

"Auntie, what do you think I've been doing?" Helen complained, "I pray all the time."

"Sweetheart, no one said that you didn't pray. However, years ago, while you were praying, the enemy began to execute plans and strategies that have been designed specifically for your family and the ministry. The level of this attack is greater than the level of your prayer life. You must pray his Word. God answers to his Word."

"Uuugh," Helen grunted in frustration. "I'm sorry. I hear what you're saying but come on. Do you really expect me to pray for this man after what he's done and is probably still doing?"

"Wake up baby! This is bigger than you and it's bigger than your pain. This is not just about Payton and what he's done. This spirit has been around for a very long time and if you choose to ignore the real issue you'll be like all the generations before you that said, my will O Lord is more important than your will. My pain is greater than your power to heal. So each generation allowed these demonic entities to rest, rule, and abide. No one has said yes to cast them out according to God's instructions. One must be willing to sacrifice his own life.

"The Word says, 'If anyone would come after me, he must deny himself and take up his cross and follow me. For whoever wants to save his life will lose it, but whoever loses his life for me and for the gospel will save it. What good is it for a man to gain the whole world, yet forfeit his soul?' This is about souls baby and prayer is your weapon. It is the most aggressive, invasive action you can take. It reaches into the spiritual realm and accesses the power of God for the circumstances on earth."

"Okay, Auntie," Helen said resignedly. "Honestly, I don't have the strength or patience for any of this. I feel like this was Payton's choice and I'm done with him and the ministry."

"Baby," Auntie exhaled and slowly asked the question again, "What did God tell you to do?"

"I don't have to ask God what to do. He clearly states in His word that there is one reason for divorce and that reason is adultery, case closed!"

"Really?" Auntie replied with raised eyebrows. "Then it's settled. There's no need for us to continue. But, remember one thing, you are a handmaiden of the Most High. At some point, because you pledged him your love and loyalty, His sovereign will, will intersect with your human will and someone has to yield. Believe me, it won't be God. If you do nothing else, listen to what He's speaking to your heart and tell Him Yes."

Helen's emotions would not allow her to grasp any of Auntie's words. "Okay Auntie, I love you. Thank you for the talk. I think I need some time to think. I'm going to the beach for a while. Do you need anything from town before I go?"

"Actually, yes. I think we could use a little comfort food. Grab that list off of the refrigerator and pick up those few things for me before you make your way to the beach."

"Done, I'll be back in a few."

25

The early, summer humidity caused a slight moisture mustache to form above Helen's top lip. The heat lingered lazily in the small, lush, beautiful town.

If the weather stays like this, I may never go home. Helen smiled thoughtfully. She had no qualms with the heat. She welcomed it with open arms after such a harsh winter.

Before Helen knew it, she steered her car into the parking lot of Rite Price Market. Approaching the first aisle, a robust voice bellowed, "That can't be little Helen? Well, I'll be, it is you." A huge Mandingo warrior of a man walked over and almost swept Helen away like a strong wind. Placing her back on her feet calmly, Jay, the owner of the store admired the woman that evolved from the small girl he once knew. "How are you Little Miss?"

"I'm fine Mr. Jay. How are you?"

"I'm just swell, Little Miss. I'm still trying to get your Auntie to let me take her out for a nice dinner."

Helen all but rolled in laughter.

"What's so funny?"

"Mr. Jay, you know how Auntie is. She's not interested in doing anything but what she is doing right now, counseling, praying, reading and teaching."

"Well Little Miss, the way I see it, everybody needs somebody."

"You're right Mr. Jay, so keep trying."

"Oh, I intend to. Put in a good word for me will ya?"

"Absolutely, it's good seeing you, Mr. Jay."

"Okay, Little Miss, I'll let you tend to your shopping. Enjoy your stay in town." Jay winked as he'd been doing for years with his toothy grin and disappeared down the third aisle.

Troubled with Auntie's words, Helen wished she could dismiss their conversation as babbling rhetoric, but she knew better. This woman had battled in prayer for years. She trusted in the Word of God and Auntie's words. She remembered Auntie saying *the Lord requires us to act in the capacity for which we were made. Always be a lady. You don't have to go mouthing off or fighting like a man. He commands his Angels that excel in strength and do his commands to hearken to His Word. All you have to do is be obedient to God's Word.*

Helen walked through the parking lot towards her car. She slowed while the clutter in her mind dissipated for a moment. "Did I get everything on the list?" She unlocked the trunk and placed the bags inside rummaging through checking the items against her list. "Okay," she said wearily. "Come on Helen, get it together." She straightened her back and slid into the front seat inhaling slowly. Exhaling, she cautiously pulled out of the grocery store parking lot. "You have to focus."

Leaning against the steering wheel, Helen began talking out loud again. "Am I really supposed to believe this mess? You can't possibly expect me to take this kind of crap. This is so foul. I'm not doing this! Absolutely not! No!"

A blaring horn jerked Helen back from her entangled tirade. "The light is not green. What is wrong with you?" She frowned at the person through her review mirror, shook her head and pulled over to the curb. "Victor, what in the world is wrong with you, man?"

"Did that startle you? I apologize. I can't believe I ran into you. I tried to call you but your phone kept going straight to voice mail."

"Oh yeah, I haven't charged my phone. Anyway, I'm trying to relax."

"Well, this must be fate. We get to hang out before I leave town."

"Victor, this is not a good time and I'm definitely not good company."

"Len, since when did that matter between the best of friends?"

"Best of friends? We are not teenagers any more, Victor. It matters."

"Come on Len, for old time's sake. We haven't seen each other for years. Let's not lose the moment."

Helen pondered the thought. "I guess. I have to drop some groceries off to Auntie's then I'm on my way to the beach. I need to sort some things out."

"Hhmm, must be heavy if you're going to the beach."

"It is to some degree."

"I'd love to hang out with you at the beach. I have to drop some contracts off first, but I can meet you in the parking lot of Jacque's in one hour and I'm not taking no for an answer.

"Fine," Helen responded airily. "I'll see you in an hour.

26

Frisbees whizzed through the air. Volleyballs pounced back and forth through raised hands and playful chatter. Children laughed running and jumping into the water to be chased and lashed at by waves. The hot sun, moist, salty air, and hypnotic ocean sounds took Helen to a place of calm and stillness where she could exhale and allow the sun to invade the dark crevices in her soul. Regardless of the noise decibel, the beach delivered serenity.

Helen and Victor walked along the sand, pants rolled up to their calves, drinking in the smell of the sea and sharing light conversation about the past. Victor finally broke through the surface.

"So what's up with you, Len?"

With half a smirk on her face, Helen replied, you don't have the time that I need to go into all of that."

"I'll make the time. You know that."

"No Victor, that's not necessary. I have some sorting to do on my own."

"Come on Len, you're working me. What's happening?"

"To be honest, I'm a little embarrassed to say." Helen inhaled and then exhaled slowly. "My marriage crashed." She inhaled and exhaled again with a long pause. "My husband had an affair. Oh, wait a minute, that's incorrect. He's had several affairs. I'm not sure how many, how long or who these women are. I stumbled onto the one that I know about."

Victor stood speechless. Helen stopped, dug her toes into the sand and looked across the ocean.   "I happened to catch him with a mutual acquaintance of ours."

"Did you confront him?"

"Yes. I sat in front of the house he was in for what seemed like days waiting for him to come out. He had no idea I was waiting outside. Long story short, he was with the Assistant Pastor's wife."

Victor's eyes widened. "What?!! Len, that's wild and way out of control. I'm not a church boy and that's out of my league." He put both hands on Helen's shoulders and gently let them fall to her forearms. "I hate to see you hurting. I'm here, whatever you want, whatever you need."

"There is nothing anyone can do. This is the most difficult thing I've ever had to face. Victor, we have a good size church. I don't know what will happen to our members? Everybody connected to us will be affected."

"Are you thinking of covering for him; just acting like nothing happened for the sake of the church members?"

"I can't do that. I won't play cover up. In the long run that will be more damaging than the sin itself. Oh God, I sound like Auntie," she said through a light-hearted chuckle. "Once you let the dog out of the yard, you have a hard time getting him back in. I believe this issue is way out of bounds. So to state it simply, I am getting a divorce."

Helen's entire being shook from the core when she made the statement. The words rolled out like the waves racing to the shore line. She swallowed hard, focusing on the streaked red sky as the sun threatened its descent. "Adultery is the one thing that I've always said I absolutely would not tolerate and you know me, Victor, I tolerate a lot. I don't need a big house or status quo cars. I've never asked for furs or jewelry. It's always been about my family and their wellbeing. What about my wellbeing?"

Victor softly touched her chin and guided her face until it met his. "Do you still love him?"

"What does that have to do with it?"

"Len, just answer the question, do you still love him?"

"I guess."

"There's no guessing. Either you do or you don't."

"Well, you don't just fall out of love after twenty-seven years, but you do make a choice as to whether you can continue to co-exist. I don't trust him and don't think I can...ever again. I find myself scanning the pews in my mind questioning the involvement of different women with my husband."

"That's understandable, but where is the Len I use to know? The girl I knew loved and loved hard. She was tenacious and aggressive. Are you really willing to throw away a lifetime?"

"Yes! No! I don't know. I hate him! Ughhhh, I hate him!" she shrieked several times.

Victor gently hugged her, "Len, stop fighting. You still love your husband. I see it in your eyes. Your emotions are raging, but I see it." Helen sighed but refused to cry. Moments went by before she realized that her arms were tightly wrapped around another man, hanging on for dear life. She felt safe and secure, if only for a moment and she didn't want the moment to end.

No words were exchanged. Helen melted into Victor's tenderness. Her firm grasp caused her to press against his chiseled form. For a moment, she had no thoughts, just a fireworks display of emotions as the syncopation of her twanging nerves burst into a crescendo of passion through short, tender kisses.

Victor immersed himself in the moment. The volcanic eruption in the pit of his stomach escaped passionately, fusing them into one. He'd loved Helen since they were teenagers; however, she never gave him the time of day on the romantic plane. He knew she was the reason he'd had several failed relationships. He compared everyone to Helen. Sure, one side of him loved variety. He'd gotten used to a buffet of delectable females, but if he believed for one moment that he could have Helen's heart, he would never engage in a female buffet again.

Helen slowly dropped her head. Shame nibbled at her conscience. Catching her breath, she looked into Victor's eyes. "I would be lying if I said I didn't want to be with you." Her voice became gravelly. Tears welled in her eyes. "Victor, it would be for all of the wrong reasons."

"Hey, hey, come on. It's not that bad. I don't mind being used."

Helen forced a smile and poked Victor in the chest, "funny. I'm sorry Victor. I'm so ashamed," she lamented turning her head to watch the sun continue its descent beyond the horizon.

"Len, the only thing I'm sorry about is..." He heaved a heavy sigh. "I must be crazy....Len, I love you, always have." Victor shocked himself not intending on expressing too much of his feelings. "This goes against every principle that you stand for. I don't want to be the catalyst that propels you into being something or someone that you're not. You'll hate me for it later and I could not bear to lose my friend."

Helen grunted, "Your friend? I've taken that for granted. You were always, always there for me Victor and it seems that you haven't changed after all these years." She held his face in her hands and kissed his cheek. "I think I took notice of your feelings too late."

"No, not really," Victor mumbled. "You were in love with Payton from the first time you met him. Remember, I could not get a word in after your first date. You bombarded me with every boring detail."

"I did, didn't I?" Helen said reluctantly. "I didn't know I was being so selfish. I would not have done that intentionally."

"It's quite alright, Len. You can't control who your heart yearns for. It's not like I'm a monk hidden away in some monastery."

"Don't I know it," Helen retorted. "I stopped counting after...what was her name...Stacy?"

"Please don't bring up Stacy the stalker." They both laughed. "Look, Len, I will always love you. Girl, God knows if I thought for a second that you'd allow me too, I'd sweep you off of your feet and take you away from everything. But, I know better. You are and will always be in love with Payton Roosevelt. You need to accept that. Come on say it with me, I love Payton."

Len coerced a smile. "When did you start having feelings for my husband, Victor?"

"You're a funny girl," Victor sneered as their arms dropped and they began to laugh out loud.

"Okay, okay, I understand what you're saying, but I've contacted an attorney and set up a meeting for when I return home. I don't think I can get past this."

"Well I'm telling you now, better yet, I promise you...," he stopped mid-sentence.

"You promise me what?"

"I need to hold on to that thought for now. Len, I'm here for you anytime; you have all of my numbers."

"I do and thank you so much for listening."

"Don't thank me. I told you. I love you, girl. Always have, always will. Now, get yourself together and try to deal with this thing before I have to start sweeping you off of your feet."

A faint smile formed, "Says you, I'm not an easy sweep."

"Don't I know it? Come on," Victor chuckled. "Let's get some food."

"I don't have much of an appetite," Helen said as she unrolled her pant legs, "but I know just the spot. Last one to the car is a rotten egg."

27

The smell of sweet potatoes and yeast rolls greeted Helen and Victor before they could walk through the door of Auntie's house.

"Helen," Auntie called with a hint of concern in her voice. "Payton has called twice already. He said he's been trying to call your cell phone since you left home, but it's going directly to voice mail. I think you should call home. It sounds pretty urgent."

"I'm sure. I'll call him in a little while. Auntie is it okay if Victor joins us for dinner?"

"There's always room at the inn," she giggled. "How you doing, baby?"

"I'm fine Auntie." Victor smiled, "I am excited that I ran into Len. We haven't seen each other for a long time. And only God knows the last time I had a good home cooked meal like this. Otherwise, life is good. May I use the bathroom to wash my hands?"

Auntie glanced over her shoulder. "Sure sweetheart, you know where to go." Victor disappeared down the hall and Auntie whispered to Helen. "You don't have the toll to cross that bridge young lady. I suggest you stay on this side of the water."

Helen sucked in her breath. "Auntie, I am not doing anything like that okay?" Auntie gave Helen the once over. "Okay baby, if you say so."

Helen sat playing with the key pad of her cell phone. Her stomach tight, she could barely breathe. "What's wrong with you? Come on, it's not that bad," she said to herself. She began dialing Payton's phone number and froze midway. Her stomach flip flopped all over the place. A small side of her missed Payton and needed to hear his voice. She needed to hear him say everything would be alright, but her pride would not allow that side to prevail. Helen continued to dial determining that she did not want to hear his voice after all. *I want you out of my life, Payton. Yeah,* she thought. *It will be better for me if I just disconnect myself, the sooner, the better.*

The voice on the other end of the phone answered, "I believe God."

"Hello, Payton."

"Hey baby, I wanted to make sure you were okay. I figured you flew down to Auntie's. There are some things going on here that you would want to know."

"Oh really? I doubt that seeing that it's your ministry and all. I don't believe I'll have much to do with any of it in the near future."

"Helen, please don't. We both spewed some very ugly insults. Can we put that on the back burner for a minute?"

Silence......."You know Payton, it's always been all about you. The crazy thing is it never mattered until now. I'm not first in your life anymore so why Payton? Why should I do anything remotely accommodating where you're concerned." Silence......

"Helen, I have some horrible news to tell you." Silence... "Well," Helen snapped.

"Helen, Tara died. She committed suicide. She drove her car to the bridge and jumped off."

"Oh, my G....." The blood drained from Helen's head and the room began to swirl. "Um, I can't imagine the pain of the family." She asked softly. "How are they?"

"Devastated. They don't understand why she would do something like this. Recently they noticed a change in her mood, but nothing that would indicate this type of action."

"When is the service?"

"Tuesday morning at eleven o'clock. Please, Helen, come back. I need you here."

Silence... "Payton, I'll see you on Tuesday morning." The line went dead.

28

Helen sauntered through the airport toward the exit. "Hi First Lady. You look exhausted. How are you?"

"I'm doing okay. Thank you for coming to pick me up, Michelle. Have you been to the church yet?"

"I was there early this morning and hear me when I tell you, something's not right. It hasn't been right for quite some time which leads me to you. What's wrong?"

"What do you mean? Your question is a little vague."

"First Lady, stop playing with me. You're different, Pastor's different, and the atmosphere is just ugly. The members are talking about all kinds of craziness. Something's happening. I can't put my finger on it, but I will say this. If this craziness has anything to do with that snake in the grass, Rachel, I will have to lay my religion down and whip her tail."

Dodging from one lane to the next, jerking and braking, Michelle looked through her rear view mirror before racing across two lanes onto her exit. "I'm about sick of Rachel. I told you when she first came that I didn't trust her and I still don't."

"Okay, Michelle. Calm down and pay attention to the road so the church won't have to deal with our funerals. Is Rachel still working at the church?"

Michelle took the opening. "Yes, she is. I heard there was some type of altercation between the two of you."

"There was no altercation. I said what I had to say and that was the end of it. She can stay as long as she desires."

Michelle ranted. "I knew she was part of the problem. I'm going to wear that tail out."

"Michelle, breathe. You will do no such thing. I've made some decisions and everything is going to be fine."

"First Lady, please tell me what's going on."

"No, not now. I don't want to talk about it. I wouldn't dare insult you by trying to make you believe everything is well, but I can't talk about it."

"Okay, I can respect that. I'll be going into my secret closet about this. I got the feeling we're dealing with some strong, defiant, ugly demons."

"Well Shel, you might be right."

29

A strange, unnatural chill moved slowly over the town unleashing a harsh wind and chilling rain. As people hurried in from the elements, a low, oppressive shroud canopied over the sanctuary. The soft musical prelude wilted beneath the sporadic outburst of devastated mourners. This would not be the typical celebration of life.

As the family and clergy processed, the wails grew more consistent. Mother Corbett sat rocking back and forth, "Jesus, Jesus, Oh Jesus. There's something else happening here. Lord, I feel it."

Mother Le Franc, Minister Harris, and others began to intercede.

During the delivery of the eulogy, Rachel sat on the side of the pulpit looking over the congregation. Arrogance oozing from her pores, she looked at First Lady and smirked. *Thought you were rid of me, did you? Take a look honey, I'm still here. You may look the part, but I know the truth. All of that elegance and poise will disappear when everything you DID NOT work for is gone. You are not fooling me sweetheart, not at all. Life as you know it no longer exists.*

First Lady sat in her regular chair, poised, back straight, legs crossed at the ankles oblivious to the snake eyes watching her every move. Her heavy heart pounded erratically. Helen shifted in her seat. *Why am I afraid?* She could not explain the unsettling panic coursing through her spirit. Pain, fear, and a very real danger swarmed around her head. *Something is seriously wrong. If I didn't know better, I'd think....* she shuttered at the absurd thought. *I'd think someone was about to storm in here and take us hostage.*

Before the final viewing, surprisingly, Tara's mother approached the pulpit to say something. A thin, Jewish woman with wire framed glasses and mixed gray hair loosely pulled back into a bun, looked out over the congregation in silence. Then she began..." my daughter, God love her, is gone. I know that God deals with us according to our hearts and I pray that He had mercy on her soul. I don't know what drove my Tara to this decision, but God knows and will deal with her and the situation according to his infinite wisdom. His ways and thoughts are so unlike ours. I have questioned Him as to how something like this could happen. Why my Tara? I will give Him no rest until He answers me and gives me peace. Presently, there is a more pressing issue to be addressed."

Tara's mother spoke slowly and deliberately, "Ladies and gentleman, there is something happening in our community, in the nation, and in the world. I would be remiss not to take the opportunity while so many of us are present to address the issue.

"People of God, evil forces are filtering through the body of Christ. Look around you and pay attention to the astounding reports of every type of abuse we can imagine happening, in the church. Greed, treachery, all types of sexual misconduct, and divorce reported nationwide at astonishing proportions, in the church. These things should not be. My Tara, God love her, took her own life and I could not stop thinking that there was a time that the power of God would have prevented this.

"I am not blaming anyone. I just want to ask one question. Where is God's power? Has he removed himself from our presence because of our selfish, insidious behavior? Has He allowed the fruits of our immoral thoughts and actions to overtake us because of our treachery? From the beginning, God set his people apart through dramatic displays of His power. Every nation knew the Children of Israel by the power and might of their God.....the Red Sea, the fire by night, the walls of Jericho, and so forth. God's testimonies remain. Where is the power of our God? It's time we look at ourselves, our lives, and what we're offering to God.

"My prayer today and I know others will join me in this request, is that the God of our Fathers will rescue us, revive us, and redeem us. May the Holy Spirit spread this burden of prayer and save us." Tara's mother slowly turned and walked back to her seat. A spark, that's all that was needed to ignite the hearts of God's people to give action to the burden of prayer.

30

Immediately after the funeral, Mother Corbett ran Helen down. "Young lady, I was determined to catch you before you ran out of here. I want you to call me, we need to talk."

"Yes Ma'am. Give me a few days to get settled. I've just returned from seeing my Auntie," Helen responded.

"Alright now, I don't want to have to come looking for you and you know I will. Now, love my neck. I've missed you." She looked intently into Helen's eyes. "Don't you do anything sudden. Be still for a little while, you here?" Helen couldn't help her blank stare. "Just say yes," Mother Corbett demanded.

"Yes Ma'am," Helen retorted. "I'll call you in a few days."

Greetings, hugs, small talk, and reminiscing about Tara. It took all of Helen's energy to make it through the Repast. She'd done well where Payton was concerned. She could barely believe it herself. Pastor and First Lady Roosevelt stood listening to countless stories. Helen leaned into Payton's side and whispered in his ear. "I'm going to go ahead home now."

"Excuse me one moment." Payton stepped away from some of Tara's relatives. "Helen, would you mind waiting for me? I'd really like to leave with you."

"Yes, I mind. I really need to go now, Payton. I don't have anything left. I'm spent."

Payton sighed, "How are you getting home? Did you drive?"

"No, I did not drive and Michelle is going to drop me home."

"Okay, I won't be long," Payton said looking at her with pleading eyes. He pulled her hand up to his lips and kissed the back of her fingers. "I'll be there as soon as I can."

Helen walked away mumbling under her breath. "No rush. I'm not sure you're going to like what I have to say."

Helen exited the side door. A tattered, old man walked across the parking lot. They passed by each other and his gazed fixed upon Helen.

"He needs you now."

"Excuse me? Are you talking to me?"

"Your father needs you now. Time is of the essence and you must do his will."

"Who's will? What are you talking about? My father is deceased. Do I know you?"

Helen turned for a moment to see if Michelle watched from the car. Helen held up her finger to let her know she would be there in a minute. When she turned back around the little old man was gone.

Helen walked towards Michelle befuddled.

"Michelle, did you just see a little old man speaking with me?"

"What little old man? Are you okay, First Lady?"

"I'm fine. Walking towards the car this little old man, the homeless sort, looked at me and said, "Your father needs you.""

"Shut up! No, he did not!"

"Yes, he did. I turned to tell you I'd be right over, turned back to him but he disappeared."

Michelle smirked. "He disappeared? Into thin air? First Lady, I think you are stressed and need some rest. I'm not saying he wasn't there but I sure didn't see him and I've been out here for about ten minutes."

"I'm telling you, he was there. Shel, what if it was an angel?" They broke out in a loud laugh, looked at each other then fell silent.

"What else did he say?"

"He said, *Time is of the essence. You must do His will.*"

"Oh my goodness, I think you just had an encounter."

"I don't know what I had. We say that the Bible is our authority, but," she took a deep breath, "I don't know. I think I need to quiet myself to see what God is saying to me. To be honest Shel, I've been running from his voice because I think He wants me to do something that I don't want to do. It's just too difficult."

"What is wrong with you, First Lady? If He asks you to do something, He gives you the power to do it, however difficult it might be."

"I guess when you put it that way, it sounds true. What if I don't want the power to do it?"

"Hhhmmm, I don't know. I believe obedience is better than anything. Don't sacrifice your relationship with God over selfishness. If you're not careful you'll run yourself into a backslidden state."

"Now how do you suppose I could do something like that?" Helen asked.

"Easy. H-e-l-l-o! Jonah, disobedience, belly of the whale, cared more about a plant than people. He slid backwards from what God wanted. We do it all the time."

"Michelle, you have an interesting way of looking at things."

"Child, don't I though. I'll be praying for you. You might as well stop running. You're not gonna get any peace until you do it His way."

"I guess. Thanks for the ride. I'll talk to you soon."

"Love ya, First Lady."

"Love you too Michelle."

31

Rachel sat in the back of Rosie's, a little hole in the wall coffee shop that made the best coffee she'd ever tasted. The walls were grungy, the booths looked like they'd been rescued from a dying diner in the seventies with a few small, round, wooden bar stools scattered about the breakfast counter. The waitress sat an order of turkey bacon, eggs, home fries, and toast in front of Rachel.

"I am so hungry," Rachel moaned.

The waitress asked clicking her chewing gum, "Anything else for you, doll?"

"No thanks," Rachel replied looking irritated waiting for the waitress to leave. Half way through her breakfast, Nina plopped down in the seat across from her. "You're late Nina. I don't like to be kept waiting. What do you want?"

"Look, Minister Morgan, I need to get rid of the DVD. This situation is too complicated. We're in way over our heads and I don't know what to do. What do you think I should do with it?"

"You're asking me because….. "

"Because this was your idea!"

"Says you! I don't know a thing about any DVD. I don't even know what you're talking about."

Nina sat stupefied. Through squinted eyes and clenched teeth, she growled in a low tone. "Tara killed herself because of you. You said I might as well make a little bit of money since I seduced her into an affair. I never thought to do anything like that until you. If anybody blames me, I'm telling everything."

"Nina, there's nothing to tell. Well, wait a minute. Let's see. There is that little secret about you liking women. Wait a minute. I don't believe that's a secret. You look like you like women." Rachel smirked. "There is also your short affair with Tara and the hidden camera recording you two in your apartment. The emphasis being YOU and YOUR. Oh and the threat of mailing the DVD to her family if she didn't give you, not me, five thousand dollars. Does that sum it up? Nina, sweetheart, you did all of the talking. There was no middle man. Tara knew nothing about me. For what it's worth, no one ever expected this thing to go this far. It was supposed to be a quick buck. Who knew she would wig out? But you, you sick, twisted freak. You pulled the punches on this one. I just made the suggestion. That being said, I don't care what you do."

Rachel paused to dab the corners of her mouth with her napkin. "Mmm, that was delicious." Rachel eyed Nina intently for a few moments. "Let me be very clear with you Nina. Never, ever, speak to me again about this situation."

Nina shuttered with rage. Rachel got up and walked out leaving her hunched over the table. Nina looked over her shoulder to make certain Rachel was gone before pulling the mini recorder from her pocket and clicking it off.

The waitress walked over clicking her gum.

"Anything for you, doll?"

"No," Nina snapped. The waitress laid the check face down on the table. Nina waited until the waitress loafed around the counter before she darted out the door.

32

"Elder Morgan, can I talk to you for a minute?"

"What is it, Maribel?"

"Well, you know what's going on around here right?"

"That's a very general question. There's a lot going on around here, as usual. What are you talking about specifically, the funeral aftermath?"

"Uuum, no Pastor Ray," Maribel whispered. "First Lady fired your wife over a week ago."

"What are you talking about, Maribel?"

"I know. She's still here. I'm telling you before First Lady went away; she came in here and told her to get steppin. When Pastor Roosevelt came in your wife was going off and I never heard Pastor respond to any body like that. I thought he punched a hole in the wall or something. Something is not right, you know. It's very strained right now and I don't know what to do. I think Pastor and First Lady are having some problems. I don't want to be in the middle of a big bru ha ha."

"Maribel, you've been working here for what, about five years?"

"Yes!"

"Then you know exactly what you should be doing. I appreciate you for letting me know. Make sure that you do not discuss this with anyone else and you need to pray for them. No funny remarks or sarcasm, just do your job. The situation will work itself out."

"So, I should be seen and not heard?"

"That's another way of putting it. Tensions are already high because of Tara's death."

"True, true, but something is wrong and I don't like it. I'm thinking about taking a few days off."

"That's up to you, Maribel; however, your discretion is very important."

"One more thing Pastor Ray. There's a woman here named Lydia. She came to see Pastor but he's not here. Do you want to speak with her?"

"Did she say what it was about?" Before Maribel could respond Ray continued, "Never mind, just send her in."

33

Ray needed to digest the poignant conversation between him and Lydia. Metaphorically, Lydia's detailed account of the church's present circumstances caused Ray's heart to race and his pressure to rise. Feelings of suffocation constricted his breathing. Lydia had not spoken of specific people, but she definitely knew the basic situations surrounding the ministry. Today after their conversation, his eyes were opened to new revelation. He reared back in his chair studying pictures of him and his wife.

"What have I done? All of these years, what have I done?" He picked up the phone and called his wife to set a lunch date. No answer. Ray felt a tug in the pit of his stomach. He jumped up and grabbed his suit jacket. "Enough is enough. Maribel, what's on my wife's schedule today?"

"She cleared her schedule to facilitate a seminar on drug abuse and addiction at the college."

With resolve in every step, Ray replied, "I won't be back this afternoon."

34

Finally, after months of planning, the City Wide Revival would take place in one week. The League of Pastors sat around the table making final preparations. Some bickered about who would expedite and preside, others, about who would preach on specific nights, and how the money would be disbursed.

Pastor Blackburn of the Methodist Church finally chimed in. "Look, we took out Sunday morning so that we all could return to our own services, preach to our congregations, and meet our church's' financial obligations. Therefore, I suggest that we pay the debts of the revival and put the remainder of the money into the League's account. We desperately need community redevelopment and we are in the position to do it. Let's get into the street. We, as the body of Christ, should have our own grocery stores, cleaners, barbershops, and salons. Come on preachers. This is bigger than just our churches. Was not this the vision in the beginning? Have we lost sight? The time to begin is now."

After a few grumblings, the majority of Pastors agreed to put the money into the League's account until the next meeting. Relieved, Payton jumped in, "okay, since we're all in agreement; let's lock down the program for each night and wrap this up, gentlemen."

35

5:30 a.m., Payton walked into his office, his mind a thousand miles away thinking on Helen. He did not notice the dark silhouette sitting comfortably on the burgundy leather sofa until he hit the lights.

"Good morning Pastor. We need to talk, today!"

"What do you want Rachel?"

"I need to know how we're going to handle what your wife knows."

"We have nothing to discuss. There is no we. You have to find another place of worship. I plan on talking to Ray today."

"Oh, so I've been your toy all of this time? A quick thrill?!! I'm not going away that easy, Man of God."

"Listen to me and listen good! Don't threaten me. I don't take threats well. I have a lot going on right now and you're not my priority or my problem."

I'm not your problem? But I've been your priority for the past year. I won't be used by you or anyone else. Now I've put my life and marriage on the line for you and your ministry and you will treat me with some respect."

"Rachel, it's over. It's been over for a long time. I don't even know how I let this happen. I don't want you, Rachel. I don't even like you. Now get over it. You have to leave the church."

Infuriated, Rachel screamed. "I will not be discarded like trash. I can do more damage than you'll ever know. You might want to re-think your position in this ménage a trois."

Before Payton could respond to another word, brute force slammed him against one of the wood bookcases lined across the wall. Books toppled, glass shattered. Payton gasped for breath struggling to free himself from the strong arm lodged under his throat.

"You slept with my wife? You, you, no good… I hope you burn in hell," Ray growled. He grabbed the bookcase directly next to him and slammed it into the floor. Ray looked at his wife cowering in the corner of the office. Eyes filled with rage, he pointed his finger toward Rachel and bit down on his lower lip instead of releasing the explicit string of obscenities lodged in his throat. Pounding the top of the desk, everything toppled before Ray stormed out of the office.

36

Rachel Morgan dialed her husband's cell phone for the hundredth time. When Ray did not answer, she hurled the phone across the room swearing when the cover fell off and slid across the hardwood floor. Nine o'clock p.m., Rachel waited alone, fretting, pining, and watching her world spiral out of control.

She looked around her office at the disarray and clutter. *Tidy up*, she told herself, picking up the mess of papers and messages strewn across the desk. *Make sure all of the clients are referred to other social workers or viable resources. Get it together, girl. You have the power to control.*

Rachel thumbed through a thick folder labeled, 'The Second Chance Rehab Center'. This substance abuse facility served as the church's primary resource for addict assistance. They were the salvation of the people. The Church assisted the Rehab Center with implementing their new roving caravan for substance abuse, offering shots of methadone to treat drug addiction.

Where is Ray? Rachel could not fathom the thought of him leaving. She sat at the chair behind her desk. *No, that's not his style. He cares too much about appearances and people. This is not how it was supposed to play out. I am not leaving! This is a long way from being over.*

Rachel thought of Helen's prissy, persnickety ways. With every thought, red, hot rage ripped through her spine.

"Poor little Helen," she whispered in a whiny tone. "Little princess that has everything and doesn't know what to do with it." Rachel spoke as if she had Helen's full attention. "You don't deserve any of it. We do all the work while you reap the benefits. I will not let it end this way. I was able to take your husband and I will take your house and your place in the ministry. Helen Roosevelt, life as you know it is over."

Rachel yanked opened her top drawer and removed a hidden tray to pull out the books that she consulted daily. She flipped through the pages until she found what she was looking for, today's date. Her sign was cancer, and lately, she felt like she was a crab at the bottom of the barrel trying to claw her way out. Today's messages read:

There are unseen forces working against you. The second read: *You are surrounded by negative karma from a previous life. Things will quickly spiral out of control.*

Rachel felt drained. She shoved the books back into her drawer and slammed the drawer shut. She booted up her computer, waited for a minute and moved the mouse to the icon she wanted. Her horoscope appeared and she let out a shrill cry. "Why am I doing this to myself? Stop it, just stop it." Her eyes fell on the blinking message:

A hostile wind has swept into your life. Prepare for a storm.

"No!" She demanded. "No, I'm in control." Rachel clicked the mouse again to read the next day's horoscope before slumping in her chair. At that moment, she noticed the purple envelope stuck under her calendar. She ripped at the side of the envelope and pulled out a note:

Minister Morgan, that's a joke. I know you. I know your kind. You are an evil, evil woman.

Her hands began to shake. Picking up the phone receiver, she dialed a number she knew by heart.

"Hello, Jamie, this is Rachel. I need an emergency tarot card reading. I know it's late, but you have to do this for me. Come on, I'll pay you extra if necessary. How much? Two hundred if we can meet in thirty minutes. You will? Oh, thank you so much. Bye Jamie."

Rachel hung up the phone and exhaled before grabbing the note and the envelope. Glancing over the wording one last time before placing it back into the envelope, she hurried to the rest room, dropped it into the sink and set the four corners on fire. Forty-five minutes later Rachel sat slumped in a chair in front of Jamie, the Tarot expert.

"Rachel, why do this again? Aren't you a Bible toting, judge and jury, Jesus believing kind of girl?"

"Jamie, I told you, God never moves fast enough for me. I am a mover and a shaker. I need things to happen now. You know what else Jamie? God is an ego maniac. Everything has to be his way. There's no flexibility with Him, just rules and regulations. But, enough about Him! Let's get on with it."

Rachel sat in the dim flickering light from a single candle. With bloodshot eyes and sweaty hair conforming to her forehead, she listened to the bleak reading.

"I don't understand Jamie. How could things turn black so quickly? Three weeks ago you told me the world was my oyster. You said the winds had turned to my advantage. Now, this?"

Jamie packed up his paraphernalia. "Things change Rachel. Good karma, bad karma, new people and old people enter into our lives. Sometimes it's a warning to get things right or sometimes it's a clear message. Do you want to talk about it?"

"No Jamie. Do I look evil to you?"

Jamie played with his words before he finally responded. "Rachel, I did not call you evil. The cards said that you have evil forces surrounding you. You need to purge them or succumb to them."

Rachel dug into her handbag. "Jamie, look, I guess I should be thanking you for doing this for me on such short notice. I'm starting to believe this is a bunch of garbage." Counting out two hundred dollars, she paid her debt.

Jamie could not wait until tomorrow. He would return to his normal job, waiting tables at the small seafood restaurant near the strip where he did not have to deal with mixed up religious nuts like Rachel.

This was just a sidebar for him, what use to be a fun way to supplement his income. He had to admit, something weird was happening. He'd never had nightmares and felt so disturbed. *What was going on in this town?* Jamie bolted the door behind Rachel and breathed a sigh of relief. Later, with a towel wrapped around his waist, Jamie took his cards, fed them through the shredder, and made a mental note to get an unlisted number in the morning.

37

Rachel let herself into the house. "Ray, are you here?" She hollered, not caring if she woke him. "Raymond!" When there was no response, she ran through the house calling his name, over and over again. Her heart began to beat rapidly. Rachel stopped when she walked into her bedroom. His closet and drawers were empty. Rachel peeked into his office which was neater than usual because everything was gone.

She sat down on the bed still wearing her coat and holding her purse. Her gaze dropped to the beautiful Persian rug, a replica of Helen's Persian rug sprawled in the middle of the floor. In an instant, she dove across the floor, sliding the rug to the side. Holding her breath, Rachel gently banged a loose floor board exposing a compact space that housed a legal size manila envelope. She breathed a sigh of relief realizing paranoia was getting the best of her.

Past midnight, time for bed. Rachel thought if she took a couple of Xanax, she might be able to relax enough to fall asleep. She ran downstairs to lock the house down when the phone rang. Spastic, she answered the phone screaming. "Raymond, where are you?"

In a calm even tone, Ray responded. "I'm where I'll be staying for the time being. I'm returning your call. What do you want Rachel?"

"Why didn't you answer my calls?"

"My phone died while I was moving my things. I had to charge my battery."

"Raymond, we need to talk."

"Rachel, there is nothing to discuss. I'm done with you."

"How can you say that? What about the ministry?"

"Ministry? You don't care about the ministry. You never have, Rachel. I knew you were selfish, but I never thought you would go this far."

"What are you talking about Ray? You don't even know what's going on."

"I know enough. It's late and I'm tired. The next time we talk, it will be through an attorney."

"You self-righteous, smug....," before she could finish her phrase, the phone went dead. "Suit yourself. I was the driving force in this marriage anyway. It's not like I'm losing much, big man."

38

Helen sat in her living room pondering the words of Tara's mother. "Where is the power of our God?" The words swam around whispering the question repeatedly in the hollow areas of her mind.

"God, where is your power? I'm so overwhelmed. I need your power, now," she blurted allowing her emotions to dictate. "I feel like I'm going to lose my mind. WHERE IS YOUR POWER?!" Helen grabbed a throw pillow and hugged it tight against her chest. Unable to utter anything intelligible, she groaned as her mind raced from one spectrum of her life to another.

Helen's countenance changed when she flashed back to her interlude on the beach with Victor. She mouthed, "I'm so sorry Lord. My heart hurts desperately. So much that I would have compromised myself and my relationship with you. Please forgive me," Helen droned releasing a torrent of tears.

"I long for Payton and then again, I get sick to think about him touching me. I feel extremely insane!!! Will I ever see him the same or respect him? Will I ever want

to touch him or allow him to touch me again? No! No!
He's a low down, dirty, dog and deserves whatever he
gets.

"What am I supposed to do? I have every right to
file for divorce, right?"

Helen sat erect and still heaving from tears. She took
a long sigh, closed her eyes and tried to breathe evenly.
"I can't live like this. I don't want to be full of anger
and resentment, but I am." A sense of absolute futility
plunged Helen into abandoning who she thought she
was or how she thought justice should be served. The
resentment that stonewalled against the demands of
her Lord began to crumble.

When there were no tears left to cry, Helen lifted her
head and a stark realization left an indelible impression
in her heart. She sat pensively for almost thirty minutes
before acknowledging the persistent passage of
scripture that disturbed her since her talk with Auntie.
'If any man will come after me, let him deny himself....'

"Okay Helen," she whispered to herself. "Embrace
it. Go ahead say it. Lay it all on the line right here, right
now." Helen felt her eyes puffing from the heavy tears.
Her face dropped into her hands as she accepted that
she must identify with the death of Christ to experience
the power of His resurrection.

For the first time in a long time, her heart, soul, and
mind said yes to God. Helen recalled Auntie's words
about two wills intersecting and one having to yield.
Today she was yielding.

The scripture continued to swell in her being, *'.....let
him deny himself, and take up his cross, and follow me.'*

Immediately Helen remembered the promise she made to the Lord, many years ago. It was just her and God when the words burned from her heart like molten lava, spewing out of her mouth. "Behold the handmaiden of the Lord, be it unto me according to thy word.

"Lord, I meant it when I said it, but I had no idea what you would ask of me. Helen lifted her head confronted with Tara's mother's question. "Where is the power of God?"

"Wow," Helen said sadly. "I get it. This unique position that I'm in is for your glory. Throughout history, you've displayed your power spectacularly through the lives and situations of your people. It seems wonderful when you're reading about it. Now that you're at my door, asking me to sacrifice my rights and my will for your purpose, I don't feel the awe of it. Can my actions really make a difference? Of course not." she swallowed. "You will make the difference through my actions."

Full of sorrow, Helen groaned heavily. "Yes, Lord. I will speak your word. Yes, I will focus on what you say and not what I see. Yes, I will forsake my way for yours. You've magnified your word above your name and your Word is forever settled in Heaven."

Scripture continued to pour from her soul. "My soul melts for heaviness, strengthen me according to your Word. Lord, plead my cause and deliver me. Quicken me according to your Word."

The muffled buzzing of the garage door opening caused an abrupt pause in Helen's plea. Her heart began to race. She took a deep breath and closed her eyes as Payton walked through the door.

39

Payton walked into the living room, which he very seldom used. "Am I interrupting your quiet time?"

"No, why do you say that?" Helen replied clearing her throat.

"Because you only sit in the living room when you're praying, reading, or having quiet time."

"True, but you're not interrupting. I am getting ready to make my way up stairs for the night."

"Before you go up for the night, I want to say one thing." Payton shifted his weight leaning against the entryway of the living room. "I said some ugly things before you left for Auntie's house. Things I should have never said. I need you to know I didn't mean what I said."

"Payton, I don't know what you're talking about specifically. A lot was said but I can't talk right now. I'm extremely tired. If you're available, we can talk in the morning. If not pencil me in somewhere."

"Why would you say that? I don't pencil you in!"

"Yes you do, mentally. You've done it for years. It just seems really harsh now because of the situation. It's okay. I'm used to it. If you can't talk in the morning, just leave me a note."

"Oh, I'll be here. By the way, you don't have to sleep in the spare room. It just doesn't seem right that you're not in your bedroom, Helen. You love your bedroom."

"Payton, it's your room too and to be honest, it's just a room."

"Now that's interesting coming from the woman who's sentimental about everything."

"Let's just say I'm learning how to wear my garments loosely."

"I hear you loud and clear. However, I'll feel better with you in your own bed, in your own room. I changed the sheets and straightened up for you. I'll take the spare."

Helen waived her hand nonchalantly. "Suit yourself."

For some reason, Payton hoped Helen would just forgive him and they would get back to life as they knew it. Then again, it didn't matter. He deserved everything she was doing and then some. He could never tell her everything. She would never forgive him.

He went into the kitchen and started a pot of coffee. "If I come clean, God will have mercy but I could lose everything. Maybe He'll touch Helen's heart and give her the grace to handle this…this… travesty. Yeah, maybe. Women are different. They forgive and love unconditionally."

Payton sat at the table with a cup of black coffee. He never drank black coffee, but tonight he needed to be awake to think clearly. Come morning Payton needed to be able to say something to his wife that would bring about a change.

Shall the prey be taken from the mighty
or the lawful captive delivered? But thus saith
the LORD, even the captives of the mighty shall be
taken away, and the prey of the terrible shall be
delivered: for I will contend with him that contend
with thee, and I will save thy children.
Isaiah 49: 24-25

40

Helen and Payton sat in the sunroom directly next to the patio. The three season room was the most serene place in the house for Helen. Tea in her hand, coffee in his, they fumbled with where to begin.

"Helen, do you want a divorce?"

"Yes," she replied coldly." Payton dropped his head pretending to sip at his coffee. "My first inclination was to divorce you. I have an appointment with a divorce attorney tomorrow morning. However, I have to be honest, I hate what you've done, but I still love you, Payton. The whole world knows it. As much as I wanted to deny it in the midst of all of this madness, I can't. You've been a good man to me most of our lives." She paused to maintain her composure. "I think you've done a lot more than what I've seen and I don't know if I can handle knowing about any other indiscretions. I believe everything that you've done will come out but I can only speak for right now. How do you propose we work through this?"

Payton's eye's slightly watered. He'd never wanted to be a disappointment to this beautiful woman sitting across from him. He adored her and it made him sick that he couldn't explain how he'd gotten off the beaten path. She looked to him like he was somebody even when he was nobody. She believed in him when they had nothing. Now, she had no faith in him at all.

"Baby, I've done nothing but think since all of this happened. I am ashamed of what I've done and who I've become. I don't know where to begin. So, I'd like for us to get some help. I am trying to clean up some business with the church and get through the City Wide Revival. Then, I suggest we leave. There's a ninety-day program out in Colorado that I've looked into for Pastors and their wives with situations similar to ours. If I get the literature will you read it?"

"I suppose. Ninety days is a long time."

"No Helen, the rest of our lives is a long time and I don't want to waste any more of the rest of our lives messing it up. I miss us, our connection, and our essence. I took it for granted and I don't know why. I know it sounds lame and childish, but…. I am sorry."

Helen sat quietly. Finally, she cleared her throat. "Rachel has to go. Frankly, I was not expecting to see her at the Funeral."

"It's done. During my confrontation with Rachel, Ray barged in. It was ugly Helen. I mean, I expected to lose him, but I…," his voice trailed off. "Ray was a superb man and I've damaged him beyond repair. I don't know how to rebound from this let alone the repercussions that are coming. When this hits the congregation, I believe we'll lose our church."

"Hits the congregation? Do you seriously believe that everyone is oblivious to what's happening? Payton, when this is all said in done, I'll be here to help you pick up the pieces of whatever is left. But, right now, I can't help you. You must make things right between you and God and whomever else you've involved. Are you going to address the church?" She paused studying his expression.

Payton's heart palpitated. He thought it would come through his chest. Afraid to stand, his face broke out into a sweat.

"Payton, are you okay?" He could not respond. "Payton?!!" Helen dropped her cup and ran over to where he sat.

He grabbed his arm. "I, I, I can't." Stuttering, Payton dropped to the floor gasping for air.

Helen ran to the phone, dialed 911, spat out the information, and then kneeled by his side to see if he was still breathing. "Yes, he's breathing, but unconscious. I think he's had a heart attack. He kept grabbing his arm. Okay, okay, hurry!"

41

The ambulance sped down the highway, rocking, lurching, and weaving through traffic as the siren blared at cars to move. Payton flat lined. Electrical paddles, clear......clear...clear, and a blip hit the monitor again. Helen realized she'd been holding her breath and almost passed out. This was the longest ride of her life.

The ICU waiting room was a cold gray, shoe box of a room with a TV mounted to the wall and eight semi padded black chairs. Helen dropped into one of the chairs and began punching numbers into the phone. "Shel, it's Helen, I'm at the hospital, and I think Pastor had a heart attack." She stopped and felt herself unraveling. Michelle spoke on the other end of the phone; however, Helen could not make out her words. The room began to spin and her hands shook uncontrollably. The phone dropped as she struggled to catch her breath. "I, I, I," she tried to speak through heaves and heavy tears. "I...don't...know, I...don't......"

A hand touched her shoulder. "Shhhh, slow down and breathe." A nursed picked up Helen's phone. "Hello, I'm a nurse here at the hospital. No, I'm not sure, but I think someone needs to get here right away."

The small framed nurse kneeled in front of Helen, stroking her arm. "There, there now, breathe. Don't try to talk, just breathe. Deep breaths, breathe in, exhale, again. There you go."

Michelle, Mia, and Maribel ran into the waiting room. "First Lady, are you okay?" The nurse gestured for them to speak calmly.

"She's better, but she needs to remain calm okay. May I speak with one of you?"

Mia walked to the side with the nurse while Michelle and Maribel attended to First Lady. First Lady sat in the chair staring blankly into space. "Pastor is in surgery as we speak. I believe he had a heart attack. I'm waiting for someone to let me know something."

Mia approached the three, looking at First Lady with fear in her eyes. "The nurse is going to see what she can find out about the surgery and get back to us as soon as she can."

Michelle spoke softly for the first time. "First Lady, a clarion call has been made for all of the leadership to begin a 24-hour prayer chain. It's going to be alright, First Lady. First Lady, look at me. It Is Going To Be Okay!"

Helen looked into her eyes and tears began to gush again. "Shel, I have to talk to my daughter. I don't know what's going to happen to her father. Oh God, what's going to happen to my husband?"

Michelle wrapped one of her arms around Helen and gently took the phone with her other hand. Mia and Maribel offered no words. They sat on either side of First Lady praying silently.

Michelle looked through the phone's address book and dialed Nesy's number. Before she pressed the button to connect, she asked Helen, "Are you ready?"

"Helen replied flatly, I'm ready."

Michelle hit the connect button and gave Helen the phone. "Hello Stefon, its Mom. No, everything isn't alright. I know it's late where you are. Will you wake Nesy for me? I need both of you on the phone. Hi Nesy."

Before Helen could continue, Nesy ranted for a few minutes about feeling something was wrong. She scolded her mother for not communicating with her or responding to her text messages.

"You're right," Helen replied dully. "There's a lot going on but I need you both to listen to me. I'm at the hospital with your father. He's in surgery right now and," she paused. "I believe he had a heart attack."

Silence…Helen continued in a monotone voice. "Nesy, I need you to calm yourself." More silence. "We're not sure of anything yet. As soon as I know something, I will let you know, okay?" More silence. "Yes, yes, I'll be in touch as soon as I speak with the surgeon. I love you too."

42

The small waiting room could not hold the many congregants now flooding the hallways and other waiting areas in support of their leader and his wife. Several hours passed. Aside from the small framed nurse scowling and directing the people from the church to a general waiting room, there was no news of surgical success or failure.

"Mrs. Roosevelt," a young Asian doctor summoned. He walked over to where Helen stood, a grim look on his face. "Mrs. Roosevelt, I am Dr. Sunkt, the surgeon for your husband, Payton. Mrs. Roosevelt, Payton has severe coronary artery disease with serious narrowing in three arteries. We performed a triple bypass, using an artery from his chest and a vein from his leg to bypass the blocked areas in his arteries. This allowed blood to flow freely to the heart. We've placed him in ICU. You will be able to see him shortly."

Feeling the heaviness in the room, Dr. Sunkt gave a short sigh. "Unfortunately, Payton is still in critical condition, therefore, only family members are permitted for ten minute intervals.

"Excuse me? Dr. Sunkt, I am not planning to leave." Helen stared at him with pleading eyes. "Please make some arrangements for me to have extended visiting hours."

"I believe we can do that for you. Everyone else will have to visit according to hospital procedures. Do you have any questions, Mrs. Roosevelt?"

"Yes...yes, I do, but I need...I need a minute."

"I understand. You may have one of the nurses page me when you're ready. Take heart, Mrs. Roosevelt. You have much support from the looks of things. We've done everything in our power. It's now up to your husband."

43

Payton's mind raced wildly. *Where am I,* he thought. Trying to will himself to move and speak, something constricted his limbs and prohibited his tongue. He remembered falling, hearing familiar voices talking, praying, and singing in the distance.

This must be a hospital, he rationalized. *This bed is hard as bricks.* Payton's eyes adjusted to the scant light in the room. Panic, dread, fear, and terror assaulted every part of his being. *I am lying on a stone altar.* Payton's heart pounded violently against his chest while fear ushered him into a slow descent to death.

"Preacher, Preacher Man, Preacher!" A mocking, sinister voice roared. His gnarled talon touched Payton's chest. "Shhhh." Payton's heart slowed and the creature continued. "There will be none of that. I'm not done with you yet."

Payton opened his eyes, his insides contorted. The creature bared his fangs. "Would you like to run? Well, Preacher, you can't." He laughed uncontrollably. "You can't move at all."

The creature's eyes brightened as he continued. "Do you think that I'm holding you against your will? Oh, contrar Preacher. Your will is what brought you here. Thy will be done, Preacher man. Sound familiar? I've whispered that to you so many times over the years. This is all your will."

The creature raised his arms high and proclaimed, "I am he that supplies all of your wants." He relished in the thought boasting about his victory. "I'm good Preacher man. My specialty is casting down chosen, ordained men with power. None of you have been as powerful as me, yet you dare to cast my kind out of man. You dare attempt to deprive me of what's rightfully mine.

"Well, another one bites the dust, Preacher. You're my latest flavor of spiritual assassin. Shall we discuss the many lives now spiritually dead from your lustful choices?" He eyed Payton tauntingly. "No? Okay, let's discuss your treachery. You are a son of perdition now. You have betrayed your God for….."

The creature's suffocating words smothered Payton's mind. *Sack cloth….ashes...no, the helper….cross…repent.* Payton's incoherent thoughts crashed and shattered against the weight of the creature's condemnation laced accusations. Guilt and shame gnawed at his temples. Payton screamed on the inside, *Help, please, somebody help me.*

…..The creature broke through his thoughts as if reading his mind. "There's no one listening to you, Son of Perdition. Did you not receive everything that you desired and more? Money, international notoriety, recognition, and women. Oh my…..the women fell at your feet by the dozens. Come on Preacher, all of that power felt good, admit it!

"Oh, the bittersweet taste of B E T R A Y A L!" The creature smirked and sang, "If it had not been for me on your side, where would you be? I never left you. I never forsook you. I waited patiently for you."

Payton, grappling with his thoughts and fighting for his sanity finally connected two small words. *Forgive me.* A glint of light flickered in his eye but the creature was too far into his discourse to notice.

Payton thought over, and over again, *forgive me.* Suddenly, a full thought crept through his mind causing the turmoil in his stomach to slightly still. *If they sin against you, and you be angry and deliver them over to their enemies, and they carry them away captives into a far land…if they bethink themselves, and turn and pray unto you in the land of their captivity….if they return to you with all their heart and with all their soul in the land of their captivity, then hear from the heavens their prayer and their supplications…and forgive your people which have sinned against you.*

Hope dropped an anchored in the middle of Payton's turmoil and he continued with tightly closed eyes and a contrite heart. *Forgive me….mercy on me.*

44

Helen sat beside the hospital bed watching Payton's chest rise and fall. Although the doctor removed Payton from the respirator because his breathing was steady, Helen felt edgy and extremely nervous. Helen desired to watch Payton through the night but fatigue rolled over her like dense fog submerging her into an exhausted sleep.

Helen's dream engulfed her immediately. She dreamed of bleeping monitors, green lines on black screens spiking and declining. Payton tangled in hospital tubing like a spider caught in a web. She jerked awake staring into the dimly lit room unable to recall the significance of the insight. Yet the sensation remained real, pulsating through her being with a conviction that she was at the doorway of a horrendous discovery.

Helen glimpsed new realities. She could feel Payton, his desperation, bound and gagged, locked in a prison without walls. Tears running down her cheeks, she whispered, "Oh Jesus, help him, please. Help us."

She fell asleep again, lost in another abstract sequence that only made sense in dreams. There were visions first as if time was speeding by, then creatures some hideous, others more beautiful than her eyes could have imagined. All of them human form, enormous, full of brute strength, spread across a great plane engaging in a fierce battle. A defenseless Payton stood in the midst of the searing battle, bound with chains.

The battlefield turned into a hospital operating room and then the church sanctuary. Helen sat in the pews along with others amidst stacks of envelopes full of cash and checks. A spot light that appeared to stream from a TV monitor flooded the pulpit which turned into a sacrificial altar. Suddenly Payton lay on the altar bound with chains.

Behind the altar, a huge door opened to blackness. Something repulsive drew near. Fear and absolute dread covered the room like a wool blanket. The beating of Helen's heart reverberated off the walls of her chest drowning out all other sounds as the hair on her arms and neck stood up. Helen clutched the ends of the pew fixing her eyes on the being. For an instant, the evil dwindled. The most indescribable man stood over her husband with a perfect physique, golden blond hair as wavy as the sea, bronze metallic complexion, and eyes faceted like diamonds casting different colors from every angle.

His alluring presence reminded every fiber of Helen's being that that she was a woman full of desire.

Clapping, hooting, and hollering! The lecherous sounds seized Helen's attention. She looked towards the choir loft where approximately thirty leaders, men, and women stood, eyes bulging. They worshipped the being standing over her husband.

A blood thirsty smile spread across his entire face. Helen approached the altar with unbelief. The being drank in every ounce of praise offered by the group in the choir stand. He walked over and stood in front of them bearing his evil grin, raising his hands in acceptance of their praise and honor. The sound heightened.

Helen expected to be overrun with emotion when she looked upon Payton. Surprisingly she was not. His chains were so in order. It made sense for him to be bound here as he had bound himself in the natural realm.

Suddenly the noise ceased and Helen broke out into a cold sweat turning to face what now was the most hideous creature she'd ever seen. His skinned turned into translucent, leather like scales. The creature's talon reached forward to touch Helen's face.

"He's mine now. It was his choice to offer himself to me after years of subtle persuasion. He was a hard nut to crack, yet, he has been cracked. This ritual that I am about to perform with him will be deemed a rite of passage to the rest of the generations following him."

He laughed a wicked laugh. "Choices, whether you make them deliberately or whether you're manipulated into making them, are still choices."

Helen could only whisper, "The blood of Jesus."

The creature roared, "DO NOT....."

She said it again louder, "The blood of Jesus," and ran up to the altar to look into Payton's eyes. In an instant, the being stood before Payton with his scaly arm lifted in the air ready to swipe down on Payton's heart.

"Payton!" The cry ripped through Helen's dry throat and she awoke to find herself doubled over in the chair. Gripping the hospital bed rails, clothes soaking wet, she cried to the Lord through wails and groaning.

Well aware of her position, Helen thought, *I look like a lunatic. I hope no one walks into this room. How in God's name would I explain this?* More groans......more sobs spewing from her belly, pouring uninhibitedly from her mouth. Beside herself, Helen gave in to the travailing. Words began to flow with intermittent groans. Helen knew she could not stop until it was over. She was not in control.

"Father, I'm crying to you in my trouble. Save us out of our distresses. Send your Word and heal us. Deliver us from our destruction. You've held your peace for a long time, you have been still and refrained yourself and now cry like a travailing woman and destroy and devour at once. Go forth as a mighty man and prevail against your enemies. Take the captive from the mighty and deliver the prey from the terrible. Deliver us from the power of darkness." More groaning. "Through your son, Jesus, all things were created that are in heaven, and in the earth, visible and invisible, whether thrones or dominions or principalities or powers. All things have been put under His feet. You're all powerful, all knowing, and your kingdom rules over all." Sobbing, "Hasten thy word to perform it." More sobbing.

Finally, able to catch her breath, Helen jumped cognizant of the stream of light filtering from the hallway. Slowly, she rose from her position to see the night nurse with a baffled look on her face. "Are you alright Mrs. Roosevelt?"

"Yes....yes, I'm fine. I'm just a bit emotional over today's events."

"Maybe I could check your pressure, or give you something to help you sleep?"

"Oh no, really, I'm okay. I'm going to sit here a while longer."

"Okay. "The nurse paused. "If you need anything, anything at all, just hit the buzzer. I'll be back to do my rounds in about fifteen minutes."

"Thank you," Helen replied sheepishly wondering how long the nurse had been standing there watching and listening to her intercessional interlude. "What does it matter?" Helen muttered as she hunched her shoulders. "It's over now."

She slowly stood teetering off balance ever so slightly. Every ounce of her energy depleted causing her to hold onto the bedrails for support. She hobbled over to her husband studying his face, tracing his brow with her finger while spiritual awareness confirmed and pinpointed the origin of their demise. Yes, the pain of Payton's treacherous actions still lingered weighing heavily against her pride, yet she knew what needed to be done.

She had to sacrifice her will, her pain, and her emotions to intercede for her husband's freedom. His life depended on it. If she did not, how many generations following would be captured and ensnared in the same manner. She thought intently then leaned over the bedrail slightly and whispered, "Hey baby. I know you can hear me. I need you to come back to me. Payton, I love you and just realized that we can't let the enemy win. We have the power of the Word to defeat him. I know you're being held captive but don't fear and don't faint or give in. The Lord will deliver you. He is sending His angels that perform his commands, responding to the voice of His word to set you free. We will declare His Word until you are freed. You must return! We have so much to live for."

She lifted her head feeling moisture against her cheek from his eyes. Helen smiled and cupped one side of his face in her small hand. "I know, I know, you love me too." She kissed his lips tenderly before leaving the room.

45

Mid-day and the church's parking nearly filled to capacity. Overwhelmed by the outpour of love, Helen sat with her hands clutched to the steering wheel trying to suck in her emotions.

"Come on girl, pull it together. You have a lot of business to handle today. You can do this." The atmosphere of the church lifted her spirit as she heard the Word pouring from the hearts of the intercessors.

First on the agenda, a meeting with the church's leaders. When Helen entered the conference room, the two elders, three deacons, and church mother were already seated around the table.

"Good morning, I mean afternoon. I'm sure you've all heard the mudslinging and rumors among the congregation." Everyone acknowledged through nods.

Helen paused and stared in the eyes of each person around the table; Elders Mitchell and Perez; Deacons Dunbar, Thompson, and Peterson; and Mother Corbett. "I've asked you all to meet me here because I need your help dealing with this...this....mess.

"I'm not too sure where to begin, but I believe that all of you have God's interest and the welfare of His people at heart.

"Let's pause on that for a moment so I can bring you up to speed. Pastor is still comatose. He has not awakened since his surgery. He is, however, breathing on his own and that's a very good thing. The other good thing…this is spiritual and God will prevail. By the way, thank you, Mother Corbett and Elder Mitchell, for rallying the church and the intercessors for the prayer vigil. From what I heard walking through the sanctuary, they've targeted the Word to fit each situation that they are aware of." More nods.

"Okay, I need your input. I'm not sure where to begin."

Elder Mitchell inserted, "Discretion and damage control is first on the agenda."

Elder Perez, chimed in, "Yes, but we need to lay everything that we know on the table so that we can execute wisely and present a unified front."

"Okay," Helen blurted. "Pastor Ray is no longer with us." Helen waited for gestures, expressions, or gasps, but the small group sat unmoved. "Just so that we are all clear, I won't ask what you've heard. I'll give it to you straight." Uncomfortable and embarrassed, she shifted her weight and her voice escalated slightly. "Pastor Ray found out that my husband and his wife were engaged in unscrupulous activity. Consequently, he emptied his office and left the keys on the desk. I have not spoken to him personally, but I share his trauma."

"Rachel Morgan was terminated. However, she has not accepted it. I understand she's still waltzing in and out of here like nothing has been communicated. How do you all think we should handle this?"

Deacon Peterson jumped in. "We'll handle it, right Deacons?"

"Right," they responded in unison. "

Deacon Thompson continued. "We'll need to get all of her keys and change the locks on the office door. We might experience some backlash knowing her, but we'll cross that bridge when we get there."

Deacon Dunbar interrupted. "Before we move to a different subject, I'd like to make an insertion." Visibly upset, he spoke solemnly. "We need to pray for and stay in touch with Pastor Ray. A hurt like that can kill a man or woman. Even if he doesn't respond, we have to let him know we care." Everyone agreed. "As for his wife, Minister Rachel, she also needs our prayers. We've all known that something has been wrong for a while. Yet, none of us said anything. She's a lost...."

Elder Mitchell interrupted. "Lost? Oh, she will be lost when I'm done with her. Then I'll pray for her. I'm sorry. I have no tolerance for deceitful women. You all can think what you want. But, I'm telling all of you, she planned this whole thing."

Deacon Dunbar jumped up flustered. "How can you say she planned the whole thing? She was not the only willing participant. No offense to you First Lady."

"Deacon please, anybody with any spiritual since would be able to see..."

"Are you saying that I have no spiritual intuition?"

"That is quite enough," Mother Corbett stated in a calm tone. "Deacon, be seated, please. We are not here to bicker amongst ourselves. There's enough of that going on in the congregation. We are here to work in concert with the Father. So, Deacons, you will handle retrieving the keys from Minister Morgan correct?"

"Yes," they all replied.

Mother Corbett looked over at First Lady and nodded for her to continue.

"Good." Helen exhaled and sat down in her chair. "Thank you, gentlemen." She breathed heavily. "Our church is in trouble. Pastor has engaged in some unscrupulous activity and we, the body, have followed him there. Outside of me and Pastor's private lives, I'm not privy to any of the other church business. I have a meeting with the church's attorney tomorrow, but make no mistake; the Lord is going to deal with it from the head to the toe. Whatever has been done, we must fix what we can on our part and repent. Judgment is eminent, however, His mercy is great. I'd like to call a solemn assembly with three days of fasting during the prayer vigil. I pray that the Lord extends his mercy and grace.

"Any other suggestions?" Helen looked around the room with wonder in her eyes.

"Yes," Mother Corbett replied. "I suggest we elect someone to act as interim Pastor until we see how things will work out."

The small group tossed their suggestions back and forth until everyone was in agreement.

Helen stood up. "I'm beginning to feel a little better. You all don't know what your support means to me. I'll be spending a lot of time at the hospital and this will be a great weight off of my mind. Elder Perez, as interim Pastor, we all expect that you will have to make some judgment calls. However, I trust that God will word your mouth and give you wisdom for this time."

Elder Perez, a Spanish fireball in his late fifties looked at Helen with great compassion in his eyes, admiring her strength and endurance. "I speak for all of us when I say you have nothing to worry about. We stand with you and Pastor regardless of the situation. May the Word of the Lord be accomplished and His will be done."

They all stood and linked hands as each leader prayed for their Pastor, his wife, family, and the congregation. After the room emptied Helen sat in the large leather chair, laid her head on the desk and sobbed.

Michelle came back into the room and placed her hands on Helen's shoulders. "I know there are no words that will make any of this feel better, but, whatever happens, whatever the outcome, know that it shall be well with you."

Helen shook her head. "Thanks, Shel. I desperately want to make it through til the end. That's the hard part. Can I really do this?"

"Yes, you can. God has called you for such a time as this. If he called you to this time, He's given you the power to obey him and walk through this valley with the shadow of death hanging over your shoulders. You'll be alright."

Helen felt like she would never be alright again. She felt beat and bruised, used and worn out, but she knew Shel was right.

46

Rachel sat in the mid-section of the church. Some people knelt, some sat, and some lay prostrate along the altar uttering, "Yes Lord. In the name of Jesus. Have your way Lord," through tears and groans in agreement with the prayer leader.

Edgy and erratic, Rachel decided to go to her office and seek her books of wisdom. Surely she'd find peace and solace from its words. Lately, her life thrashed about like a hurricane and all she wanted was shelter from this storm.

The tinkling of her keys jiggling the lock, Rachel's arm pits began to sweat. "What the…." She never noticed the two Deacons standing behind her.

"Minister Morgan, we need your keys to the church."

"What?!! Why?!! No! Who changed my lock and what's going on?"

"Minister you'll have to take that up with Elder Perez."

Her arms flailed. She ranted, "You will unlock my office, now!" Rachel dropped the keys and Deacon Thompson scooped them up instantly removing the church keys.

"Here you go," he responded dryly handing her the key ring. They escorted Rachel to the back door, each Deacon on either side of her with a slightly firm grip.

"You have no idea who you're dealing with. I'm going to sue the church and you for putting your hands on me."

Okay Minister, have a nice day." They closed the door and stood in front of it.

Irate, Rachel spat, "Oh no you did not. I am the wrong one! You wanna play rough? I can play rough."

47

Helen whizzed across the highway to the hospital exit. The incessant buzzing of her phone reminded her to check her missed calls. She pulled into the parking garage, began pressing buttons on her phone, scribbling onto a piece of paper.

She punched in the first number. "Hello Raymond, I'm returning your call. I know the place. Yes, we can meet. I'll see you tomorrow morning, 9 am."

She punched in another number. "Hi, Nesy. I got your flight information and I'll have someone pick you up from the airport and take you to the house. Daddy's condition is still the same. Call me when you land. I love you."

Everything seemed to be going so fast. Helen felt as though she was losing control. She punched in one last number and talked for thirty-five minutes. By the time she hung up from Auntie, she felt like new life had been breathed into her body.

48

Rachel looked bug eyed and wild with fury pacing her living room like an agitated alley cat. Frantically punching numbers in her phone, she willed Jamie to answer. He could give her a card reading and tell her what to do. She stopped dead in her tracks when the phone jingle began. "The number you have dialed….is no longer in service."

Rachel barked, "You would do something like that Jamie. You're such a wuss."

She closed her eyes and took three long, deep breaths. "I can do this," she whispered after centering herself. Rachel fought images of her former spiritual family skulking in her mind.

She met them during her freshman year of college taking a course in New Age and Intuitive Studies. The unique group of people known as 'The Cell' was the catalyst that thrust Rachel into occult activity. The fascination with their ability to make things happen and manipulate matter through concentration and meditation won her over. In the beginning, Rachel had been tenacious in her studies and attendance. She desperately sought to command the type of power that 'The Cell' wielded. After graduation, Rachel's attendance became sporadic drawing the conclusion that she learned enough to get what she needed and wanted.

Rachel shook her head to crumble the faces and memories in her mind. She carefully removed the medium sized leather parchment book from the manila folder that was hidden under the loose floor board. "Since Raymond is no longer here, I don't have to hide you. He never understood my power and abilities."

She continued to speak as if engaged in conversation with another person. Rachel turned methodically pulling the shades over the wide rays of light pouring into the windows. Finding the correct page, she sat on the floor, legs crossed, eyes closed, hands resting and palms up. Rachel's chant began inaudibly. Within thirty minutes, the incantation grew louder with more passion and concentration until the atmosphere of the room changed and a presence slithered through. There were only a few other occasions, during group settings, where Rachel obtained this heightened spiritual state. However, she had never been alone. A tinge of fear crept up her back. She continued the incantation. The warmth of what felt like an embrace wrapped around her body and a faint smile formed at the corners of her mouth. There was no audible voice, yet Rachel could hear loud and clear.

Have I not promised that all would be yours if you would worship me? Yet your brothers have cast you away.

Rachel listened and responded. "Yes, I will do your will. Yes, my Lord."

49

Irritated by every sound that seemed magnified one hundred times over, Ray looked beat up, distressed, perplexed and unshaven. As Helen approached the table, Ray ran his lumberjack sized hand across the scruffy shadow on his face and wondered how she did it? She looked exquisite.

"Hello, Raymond." Helen sat down coolly. "What can I do for you?"

"Helen," Ray kept his eyes glued to the manila envelope sitting on the side of his plate. "I'm sorry that I have to do this now. I've wrestled with what to do with this information and honestly, the only thing that keeps me from exposing it all is the fact that I am linked with it. I almost didn't care since that haughty....." He stopped and took a minute to compose himself. "I'm sorry, that's the last thing you need to hear."

"Ray, we're kind of in the same boat. We both saw, refusing to see. We heard, refusing to hear, all the while making a silent choice of agreement with Payton's actions. I've come to accept that he is just a man full of flaws. Does that excuse his actions? By no means, but Ray we should have done our part. We did not make Payton accountable and for that we're wrong. We all must deal with our issues."

A waitress appeared, took their orders of coffee and tea and scurried away. "How are you and Rachel?"

"There is no me and Rachel. I'm filing for divorce."

"I'm sorry, Ray."

"Don't be," he lamented. "Everything that you just said equally applies to my relationship with my wife. She's a malevolent person and I refused to acknowledge that for a long time. Now I'm paying for it. Such is life, right? What about you and Pastor?" Ray asked almost choking on the odorless sludge that formed at the back of his throat making him want to spit every time he said the word, Pastor.

"I can't leave my husband, Ray. Nothing can be solved that way. Besides, this vicious cycle must be broken."

With callous eyes, Ray retorted, "Oh, so you'll put on your super cape and save the day, right? Oh, wait a minute. Let's not forget the God factor." Holding up one arm like a super hero he spouted, "For the saints of God and the Lamb!"

Helen offered a faint smile. "You know Ray; I understand your cynicism, really. I fight myself every day to focus on believing what I know God said. I have more reason than most to believe that this entire Christian experience is a farce, but I can't deny my personal experience with God or the things He's revealed to me." Helen's eyes grew heavy. "It's time for me to own up to what I know to do and allow God to handle the rest." Helen paused as if in deep thought. "I thought I loved God, Ray. I believed that I was doing his will diligently and dutifully as the First Lady of Spirit and Truth. Now, in the midst of the worst pain I've ever experienced, I realize my love for Him was, at best, shallow. I see where I should have made stands for righteousness.

Ray watched Helen's face grow weary. Toiling with his own inner struggles, he dropped his defenses for a moment. "Yeah, I hear what you're saying. I just don't think I can do it anymore."

"Do what anymore, serve God?" Before he could answer, Helen continued. "Were we really serving God or promoting a vision that was God inspired, and then became tarnished when left unchecked according to his principles?"

"Honestly Helen, I don't know anymore. I have a lot of soul searching to do and I plan on taking a lot of time to do it."

Helen placed her hands over Ray's right hand resting on top of the envelope. "Ray, we've known each other for a long time. You're like my family. Please believe me when I say I'm so sorry for you and your family. You are a good man and I pray that you don't allow the flaws and actions of one man to undermine your relationship with God."

Ray looked at Helen exhausted and defeated. He slid the envelope in front of her and pushed his chair away from the table. "I think it's too late." He laid fifteen dollars on the table. "Do what you think best with this information. I hope things work out for you."

50

Helen, accompanied by Elders Perez and Mitchell, sat in the modestly decorated corner office of Myron Wright, Spirit and Truth's legal counsel from Wright, Wright, and Thurman Law Firm. The success of this great law firm could not be measured by appearances.

Helen wondered how she would swallow the meal that Myron was about to serve. She'd just found out that the church added fictitious names to the roster to balance the large sums of money or what looked like large gifts donated to the ministry.

"Good morning Helen. You're looking well as always. How is Pastor Roosevelt doing?"

"He hasn't come out of the coma yet Myron, but his condition is stable. Thank you for asking."

"Good morning Elder Perez, Elder Mitchell. Helen has made me aware of your roles with the ministry at present. I'd just like to reiterate that what we will be discussing today is of a very delicate nature."

Elder Perez responded before Myron could finish. "We are well aware and will conduct ourselves and the business of the ministry accordingly."

"Well," Myron said, "There's a lot of ground to cover and no time to ponder over decisions. We must define our actions by the end of this meeting." Helen glanced at the others and then gave Myron a slight nod.

They listened intently, sitting stoically as Myron apprised them of one situation after another.

Myron finally concluded. "The church needs to settle two real estate cases currently under investigation because the properties were purchased from the families below market value. The original intent of the sale came about to assist the families out of financial distress. However, something went awry and the equity was taken from the properties leaving both families in an increased state of financial deprivation, resulting in bankruptcy. The Trustee over the cases agreed to settle one estate for seventy-five thousand dollars and the other for one hundred twenty-five thousand dollars. If the cases are not settled out of court, the church along with the church officials involved will face harsh scrutiny and maximum penalties. If we comply with the settlement offer, the church will maintain ownership of both properties."

Myron slowly poured water into his glass allowing the group time to digest his words. "The church is presently a partner in a ministry known as Kingdom Ministries. Are you aware of this ministry or the people involved?"

Elder Perez replied blankly, "We're aware of the leaders involved and its existence, but that's it."

"Okay, Kingdom Ministries is an international ministry with its center of operations located in Amsterdam. The Kingdom has raised large sums of money through multiple streams. They've taken their large sums and turned a rather substantial profit over the past five years. My sources found that the profits have been gained from high stakes gambling, a small prostitution ring, and a marijuana operation that funds the Kingdom's 'Spiritual Guru' at the helm. While these activities are somewhat acceptable and legal in other countries, in this country, the church will be prosecuted to the fullest extent of the law.   Mrs. Roosevelt, your husband has been sleeping with the enemy, per se.

Helen never blinked, but thought, *you have no idea.*

Myron continued, "In my opinion, the church needs to disassociate itself from Kingdom Ministries and fix the accounting issues before things escalate or get exposed and criminal charges are filed. This firm is working vehemently to control the damage. I've called in a few favors and feel confident that we can contain the situation." Myron sat quietly again for a few minutes, hands folded on the gray metal desk. "This is a lot to ask you to decide on such short notice, but we have to do it. What do you think?"

Helen had no idea when the sudden insight invaded her thoughts, but at that moment she knew outside of the praying and the fasting, they had to take action now. The house had to be set in proper order beginning today. She stood and subconsciously whisked the wrinkles out of her skirt. "Elder Perez, if you don't mind I'd like to speak for the ministry first. Because this began with my husband, I feel the need to settle it for his sake."

"By all means, First Lady."

"We will sever all ties and associations with Kingdom Ministries. As far as the real estate is concerned, pay the court settlements and offer each family their home on the terms of the original agreement. If they are not in the position to take the homes back, you may offer them the amount of equity that was taken from the properties as a gift. It has to be one or the other, not both. Helen asked resolutely, "Are we clear?"

Myron wobbled around the gray metal desk with a look of satisfaction on his face. "Crystal. It's as good as done. Any questions?"

Everyone answered collectively, "No."

Myron extended his hand. "Elders, I bid you God's speed in assisting the church. Helen, it's always a pleasure."

51

Rachel skidded to a stop in front of Nina's house crazed and ready to destroy. She sprinted up the steps banging on the door and hollering. "Nina, Nina, open up. Come on I know you're in there."

Nina cracked her door. "What! Didn't you tell me never to speak to you again?"

"Oh Nina baby, come on, you know I was just playing with you. We're a team you and I. Besides you know I wouldn't hang you out to dry like that." Pushing her way through the door, "Let me in. We have some business to discuss."

Nina raised one eyebrow, "What's up? You fixin to use me again? I don't think so."

"Nina baby, listen to me." Rachel grabbed Nina by the hand and led her to the sofa to sit down. Her demeanor calmed as she stroked Nina's hair. "I'm sorry about Tara. We did not make her do what she did. It's obvious there was some pre-existing issue.

Rachel swallowed hard and looked into Nina's eyes. "Nina, Ray and I are done. All I have is you. I need you." She searched Nina's eyes for a speck of hope. "Don't leave me like Ray did, Nina. I can't be alone right now."

Nina slowly withdrew her hand from Rachel. "How do I know that I can trust you?" Nina was very aware and a little afraid of Rachel's dark side.

"Like I said, Nina, you're all I've got. Will you do this one thing with me? This is it. I promise."

Nina hated the influence that Rachel had over her, yet, she could not resist. She gave in. "Okay, let me hear it."

Rachel hugged Nina and whispered tenderly in her ear. "You won't regret this." Immediately, Rachel jumped up pacing in front of the leopard sofa. "I've gathered some information that's a sure shot."

"Who's the innocent sucker this time?" Nina spat sarcastically.

"It's not exactly who, it's more like an organization that snubbed its nose up at me and I want to settle the score."

Nina did not like the sound of this already. She folded her arms. "I don't know? Look at what happened to Tara. What if this blows up in our faces?"

Rachel sang, "Not this time. We're talking two hundred fifty thousand dollars easy. That's enough for us to get out of here and start fresh." She walked over to Nina, grabbed her hands again and pulled them close to her heart. "You don't have to say a word to anyone. This is all you have to do and I'll do the rest."

Nina listened. Her eyes grew wide and she pulled away from Rachel. "Are you on drugs? You must be smoking some serious stuff. I may be dumb and wild at times, but even I know when to draw the line."

"Nina, I attended the church and they handled me. They took my stuff, put me out and slammed the door in my face. These people are brutal. They don't care about you and they certainly don't care about me. They serve their own interests. I've been on the inside for a long time and believe me they got it coming. They manipulate and exploit the weak. After you're all used up, they discard you like trash. Ask me how I know? I just want to give back everything they've dished out to me all of these years."

Nina couldn't respond. Rachel continued, "They're all in it for the money and the lavish lifestyle. That's the nature of the beast. All I need you to do is make the drop and I'll take care of the rest. Think about it, two hundred fifty thousand dollars, me, you and a new start. It sounds so good, doesn't it?" Nina shook her head in agreement.

52

The City Wide Revival had come and gone with
great deliverance. Yet at the Roosevelt residence,
slumped around the board room table located in the
conference room at one end of the house were seven
leaders of Kingdom Ministries.

Elder Perez and First Lady Roosevelt stood
uncompromising at opposite ends of the conference
table accompanied by Spirit and Truth's newly
appointed row of counsel: Elder Mitchell, Deacons
Dunbar, Thompson and Peterson, and Mother Corbett.
Helen's daughter, Nesy, stood near the double doors
with fire and fight in her eyes.

At the other end of the house, the family room
closed off by see through French doors blocked with
heavy drapes had been turned into a make shift
hospital room for Payton. Still, in an unexplained coma,
the family doctor visited each day assuring Helen and
Nesy that this sort of thing happened from time to
time. Oftentimes, people did not wish to wake up from
sedation. This phenomenon occurred sometimes when

surgery patients awakened in the middle of surgery, experiencing the horror of pain or blood. The trauma keeps them unconscious long after the effects of the sedation have been eliminated from the blood stream.

Nesy agreed with the doctor, but to Helen, the explanation remained supernatural. There was nothing physical about Payton's state. He remained comatose because he lay, still bound in the invisible realm of the spirit. A physical therapist worked Payton's limbs every day to keep his muscles from atrophying and blood samples were taken to try to determine a cause for his comatose state. Nothing had been found.

After scrutinizing over all of the documents now sitting in a neat pile at the corner of the table, Elder Perez peered at the seven leaders of 'The Kingdom'.

"Pastor Raymond Morgan has resigned as the Assistant Pastor of Spirit and Truth and Operating Officer of 'The Kingdom'." Tapping on top of the mountain of documents, Elder Perez continued, "He has given First Lady Roosevelt Power of Attorney and apprised her of the business dealings thus far. Before First Lady Roosevelt addresses you I want to say that we've had to make some hard decisions over the past few weeks. We solicit your full cooperation and support." He gestured for First Lady to take the floor.

Reaching for a green folder, Helen opened the folder, looked over the documents for a moment and asked, "Can someone please explain the Rescue and Revive Fundraising letter?"

A stout young man that had been part of the ministry for four years shot a glance at the others before speaking. "It's a fundraising letter with a response device attached geared towards anyone who is, knows, or is connected to substance abusers."

"What is the response device?"

"The response device is anointed oil, prayed over by our intercessors to be used on the substance abusers for deliverance."

"So what you're saying is The Kingdom purchased thousands of these little vials of oil and had the intercessors pray over them specifically for deliverance from drug addiction? All, for a small donation?"

"Well yes and no." The young man looked perplexed. "The supporters get the oil whether they send a donation or not. This is also coordinated with the Rescue and Revive Internet Bible Study hosted by each Partner of the Kingdom from month to month."

"I see." Helen paced with her finger resting on her chin. "Now, regardless of the nature or intensity of the drug addiction, we are telling our subscribers that this vial of oil is the answer?" No one responded. "Good answer. That was a rhetorical question. Can anyone tell me how many fundraising letters have been mass produced and mailed that yielded profits?"

A young Asian woman with gold wire framed glasses, and silky long black hair, spoke firmly. "Four letters over two years focusing on different areas of deliverance with the response devices geared directly to the specific areas of deliverance. For instance, pornography. The letters have yielded the Kingdom approximately nine hundred fifty thousand dollars." She continued confidently. "The Kingdom tithed ten percent of that to the headquarters in Amsterdam. Once a year, Amsterdam sends a return check ear marked for Community Redevelopment to each participating ministry of the Kingdom. The check is based on the amount of money that remains after operating costs have been met."

"Well, thank you, Ling. How impressive. You should give yourselves a hand." At that, the small group began to exhibit signs of relief and renewed confidence. "You know; I would have never thought that 'The Kingdom' operated on such an excellent business level. I can say that you all have done a splendid job financially. However, I'd like to share some other Kingdom business with you."

Helen's tone remained stark. She picked up a manila folder and dropped it in the middle of the table. "According to Myron Wright, Spirit and Truth and the Kingdom's legal representative, The Kingdom in Amsterdam have been investing in high stakes gambling, prostitution and a thriving marijuana business that supports your spiritual guru, um, um, whatever his name is." She paused for affect. Chaos rode in upon her words grappling at the minds and tearing apart all thoughts of the supposed innocent business practices. "Certainly all of you are aware of the thousands of fictitious names of families and individuals used to substantiate the large checks that you've received over the past few years? Surely you all know that should this information become public, Kingdom Ministries and each one of you will be investigated and prosecuted to the fullest extent of the law."

Heavy sighs and groans filled the atmosphere. One of the leaders broke out into a wail. "I'm not going to jail. I followed orders specifically."

Helen looked solemnly. You are responsible for your own actions. Now, we don't know if anything will come of this. Our law firm is working diligently to contain any damage that may have leaked out. If the media gets wind of this and you all know how that can go, it will blow The Kingdom as well as Spirit and Truth out of the water."

Helen purposely continued without giving the leaders time to process her words. "You are all fired!" The board sat frozen. No one breathing or blinking, just listening. "Kingdom Ministries in this small corner of the world are defunct. You may remain with Spirit and Truth as members if you so choose, however you will never be given the opportunity to serve in a professional capacity again. You are to discuss these findings with no one as it will only cause detriment to you if this turns public. Are we clear?" Some nods, mumbles, and grumbles.

The stout young man gave a long exhaustive sigh. "You couldn't be any clearer, First Lady."

Helen gestured to Elder Perez. "Anything else Elder?"

Elder Perez spoke pleasantly. "I think that covers it. Thank you all for your time. Nesy will show you to the door."

53

The chilly, blustery day full of thick, gray clouds attested to the storm looming on the horizon. Nesy saw the last of the Kingdom administration to the door and her mental alarms began to screech.

Hurrying down the hallway back to the conference room she called out, "Have you all seen the weather conditions?"

Before she could finish, Nesy cut herself off at the sight of her mother crying. A mixture of parents, the full bodied, medium brown skin, pronounced afro centric facial features, and sassy short haircut Nesy rushed to her mother's side. "Mommy you did well. Please stop crying or you'll make me cry."

Helen lifted her head and smiled through glassy eyes. She kissed the back of Nesy's hand and held it to the side of her face. "Thank you all so much for your support. These are tears of joy. For the first time in years, I know in my heart that I've…..we've done the right thing."

Before she could continue, Elder Perez began to dance a jig and Elder Mitchell broke into a hearty laugh.

"First Lady, you did the sure nuff thing. Good God, I knew you had it in you."

"Honey," Mother Corbett joined in. "I wish we could have spoken for you, but you had to do this because of the nature of this situation. You did a stupendous job."

The Deacons smiled with acceptance. "We concur."

With an invigorated spirit, Helen straightened her back, clapped her hands, and raised them high. "Thank you, Lord. Whew, thank you, Lord. It feels so good to be obedient to Your will." She tried to calm herself but sheer exhilaration caused her to spring out of the chair. She paced from one end of the room to the other. "We are just beginning. I don't know how the Lord will move, but move He will. He will respond to his Word. Okay, okay, subconsciously tucking her blouse into her dress slacks, I have to calm down, but I feel so free."

Everyone felt the weight of the sin lifting. They basked in His presence, in newness, and in freedom. Helen finally continued. "We don't know what to expect in the near future as far as the misconduct of the Kingdom, but I'm sure the Lord will navigate us through it. I believe we need to put a permanent row of counsel in place for Spirit and Truth. Including each of you, we need names to pray about adding to this number."

Everyone agreed that Pastor Roosevelt, should he recover, be subject to this row of counsel and they likewise are to be subject to him.

Elder Perez quipped, "No more stealth maneuvering is alright with me. I mean, no ruling body is perfect, but accountability gives less chance for foul play."

"Absolutely," Deacon Thompson agreed. "But, I think we've done enough for today. Let this sink in. First Lady, relax. Sit with Pastor. While there is a lot to be done, let's pace ourselves and continue to seek his face. I for one am looking for Pastor to wake up and do what needs to be done to set the house in order. I understand full well the level of damage that's been done, but, let's not forget that this same man led us passionately, fired by the Holy Spirit for over twenty years. We've seen the fruit of his labor." They all nodded in agreement.

"Well said Deacon," Elder Perez responded.

First Lady hugged everyone. "Thank you again, all of you. Before you leave, poke your heads in to see Pastor."

Babbling and basking in new freedom, the small group made their way to the family room to peek in on Pastor Roosevelt before leaving. Nesy opened the door to her father clearing his throat. His hand moved across his face and slowly rubbed his eyes.

"D a d d y!" Nesy squealed barreling through the door.

When Payton removed his hand, he found himself face to face with the tearful eyes and awed expressions of Elders Perez and Mitchell, Mother Corbett, and Deacons Dunlap, Thompson, and Peterson. He scanned the room under the bear hug of his daughter. "Nesy?"

"Yes, daddy? I'm so happy you're awake."

"So am I, baby. Now if I could only breathe."

She giggled and raised herself from the bedside. Payton's eyes blinked furiously trying to focus to see around the jubilant bunch. "Where's Helen?"

They all moved aside to reveal a teary eyed Helen with hands clasped over her mouth and heart racing.

"Oh God," she whispered. "Oh my God, Oh my God, you're free. God is doing just what He said." Helen spoke under her breath. Mother Corbett pushed her towards the bedside.

Helen touched the side of Payton's face lightly. Their eyes glistening sharing new found freedom.

Payton whispered into Helen's ear as she leaned over him in an embrace. "Yes baby, I'm free. No one will ever understand."

Helen lifted her head and looked directly into his eyes. "They'll understand because we must share it."

"Yes we must." He smiled, "and we will."

54

The flutter of wings jerked Nina out of her stupor.
One hour before the designated time for her to
implement the plan. Two hours before the evening
news with Bryce Owens.

Nina paced the walkway in front of the small library
trying to decide if she really wanted to go through with
Rachel's craziness. *Something did not feel right. Pay
attention to your gut,* she thought, lighting a black and
mild. *The last time it cost a life.*

Images of Tara's car stopped mid span on the bridge
struck at Nina's conscience. The reporter's words,
"committed suicide," reverberated in her mind. Nina
constantly fought her thoughts finding solace in
drinking. However, lately, Hennessey was not able to
thrash away the image of a floating, limp, Tara, faced
down in the murky water. Nina blinked furiously as if
scrubbing the impression away.

She sat down on the steps, inhaled long and hard, exhaled and continued mulling over questions. *What will these people say about me? They're seeing my face, not Rachel's. Will I really be an anonymous source?*

Nina flicked her cigarette butt into the street and carefully considered the package under her arm. She started across the street towards her destination and a wave of panic crashed against her chest. "Come on Nina, pull it together. You've never backed down from anything."

Nina thought about Tara again. *Ready or not, here I come.* Nina walked towards the newsroom knowing that after today, her life would never be the same.

55

A brutal storm swept through the city. Gale force winds, golf ball sized hail stones, continuous rolling thunder, and lightning strikes caused fires everywhere. Everything shut down as flash flooding raged through communities. The devastation seemed insurmountable.

Payton and Helen sat listening to reports of fires and massive damage ravaging the neighboring areas around the church. Finally, Helen turned off the transistor radio they found rummaging through the basement while preparing for the storm.

"Payton, it's been two weeks. We've avoided conversation long enough. You need to know what took place during your coma." Silence…. "Whether you're ready to deal or not, Kingdom Ministries could be brought up on drug charges, prostitution and God knows what else. Myron is doing his best to get us through this unscathed, but realistically, we should prepare for the worse.

"Payton," she paused to catch her breath. "Everything that we've worked so hard for has been in preparation for a future that may not exist. You could be brought up on charges. I could be charged as an accomplice just because I'm married to you." More silence. "I know it seems like we're drowning but I can't help but think of the many, many lives that have been devastated locally and internationally."

Settling down on the sofa, Payton dropped his head into his hands and wailed. After a time, he lifted his head. "Helen." He spoke through raspy breaths. "I'm constantly plagued in my mind with that very thing." His voice low and hoarse, Payton stuttered. "The many lives crippled, maimed and destroyed because of my….," he swallowed hard, "my selfishness and greed. I don't know how to live with that. I've asked God to forgive me but I don't know how to forgive myself. I spiraled out of control. Babe, I started out with pure motives and somewhere along the way, the pressure to keep up with other ministries sucked me into a fast, furious whirlwind.

"The Kingdom offered me status and prestige. With the status, came women, different nationalities throwing themselves at my feet. I know you don't want to hear this but I have to say it, so please bear with me. The Kingdom is a door I should not have walked through, but the seduction overpowered me. I would finally have an international ministry, my own air transportation, and televised broadcast, all without the great struggle."

Payton shook his head vigorously. "Before I realized, I'd gone too far and didn't know how to get back." He grimaced. "My idolatry erected a high place and I have to tear it down. If I don't, it will affect our grandchildren and their children. God knows I do not want to get convicted and serve jail time, but if that's where the truth is going to take me," he swallowed hard again and paused, "then so be it.

"I thought I was going to die at the hands of that savage beast. The terror, taunts, and ridicule that I experienced is something that I can't begin to describe. I never want to be enslaved by sin again. Ironically, with all of my studying and preaching, I didn't get it. I under estimated the power of the enemy and overestimated my ability. I thought more highly of myself than I ought. It was almost the death of me."

Helen sat quietly and wondered, *Lord, how can I be sure that he's sincere? God, only you know his heart, please show me if he is really sincere.*

Payton continued, breaking through her thoughts. "Helen, it's too much power for one man to run everything and make all of the decisions. There are too many temptations, traps, and distractions. I think every leader needs some sort of counsel. You know like a circle of people with a heart after God."

"Excuse me?" Helen sat on the edge of her chair astonished by what she just heard. "Repeat what you just said, Payton."

"What? Every man needs a circle of counsel? You know like the scripture in Proverbs says, 'in a multitude of counselors there is safety'. I get it now."

Helen arose from the chair, knelt down in front of her husband gazing into his eyes. "There you are, welcome home baby. I do believe with God's help we can make it."

Payton smiled, "What did I say?"

She hugged him and whispered, "The truth."

56

Finally, the sun sliced through the clouds after four days of cyclonic like devastation causing a great loss of people, property, and power. Payton's cell phone buzzed most of the morning.

He answered, "I believe God.

"Top of the morning to you Pastor Roosevelt. Can you talk?"

"Well, Myron that depends on what kind of news you're toting."

"I'm afraid the news is not favorable. As we speak, one of your members, Rachel Morgan, is being apprehended for extortion. The other woman involved, Nina Jamison, will be charged but probably given leniency for cooperating with authorities."

"Who…what? Did you just say extortion?" Payton moaned. Flustered and deflated, the pit of his stomach fluttered.

"Well, it seems that Ms. Jamison waltzed into the Police Station with some incriminating Church documents. The documents were to be given to a reporter if the church did not acquiesce to a two hundred fifty-thousand-dollar demand. While Ms. Jamison chose not to use the documents against the church, she did confess that Rachel Morgan approached her regarding this scheme and she has it on tape. She also confessed that she and Rachel drove Tara Rubenstein to suicide."

Myron paused. "Apparently Ms. Jamison instigated a brief affair with Ms. Rubenstein. She recorded the two in an act of intimacy and threatened to send a copy of the recording to her family if Tara refused to pay five thousand dollars. Ms. Jamison states that she also has tape recorded proof that both she and Rachel Morgan were involved. However, according to Ms. Jamison, they did not expect Tara to kill herself.

Silence. "To put it lightly Pastor Roosevelt, the stuff is about to hit the fan. The church will not be able to dodge the media once this seeps into the airways. Prepare yourself and the ministry for some very intense scrutiny. That's the bare bones. I won't have complete details until the inquisitions are over."

Payton felt like his lips were cemented together.

"Pastor Roosevelt, are you there?"

"Uh, yes Myron. I um, wasn't ready for that."

"I know. I wanted to prepare you before the eruption. I'll be in touch."

"Thanks for the heads up, Myron."

Helen walked into the room. "I'm ready." She did a double take. "Payton, what's the matter?" His face appeared ashen. He sat Helen down and conveyed the news.

Helen sat speechless with a blank stare. "So it begins. Payton, this might get really ugly."

"I know. I have to face it, though. I can't cover up anymore." Payton pulled Helen close to his chest. "I'm so sorry. I pray that God protects you in the midst of all of this. I was so foolish. God, please don't charge me my life," he pleaded. "I am guilty. I repent. Please, show me how to navigate through this dangerous water."

Payton and Helen stood embracing each other for some time. Helen exhaled. "We have to go. We need to get this over with."

"You're right," Payton sighed. "It's now or never."

Helen grabbed her bag. "Do you think we should stop by Tara's mother's house first?"

"No, let's allow the authorities to contact the family first."

"I'm not sure if I'm ready to see the Church Payton."

"I know baby, me either. Let's go before we talk ourselves out of it."

After three hours of traffic and detours, the Roosevelts pulled in front of what used to be Spirit and Truth Family Worship Center. Overwhelmed at the sight of just the church sign, charred remains, and rubble, they fell into each other's arms and cried. Members of the congregation began to appear in droves. Disbelief and utter chaos permeated the grounds.

Payton released his wife and turned to face the congregation.

"Saints, I need to speak some truths to you today." He grabbed First Lady Roosevelt's hand and intertwined his fingers with hers.

"The natural devastation that you see is equally devastating in the spiritual." Puzzled looks, gasps, and murmuring waved through the crowd.

"Because of some of my choices....because of my disobedience....my arrogance and pride, we are ensuing upon cataclysmic circumstances.

Over the next few weeks, allegations may be made and stories will be told. Some will be true, some will not. However, for everything that you've heard and everything that you will hear, I am sorry. I have repented before God and I now repent before you."

Payton's heart sank as the crowd thinned. He squeezed Helen's hand waiting for the movement to stop. After the movement settled, approximately one hundred people stood before Pastor Payton and First Lady Helen Roosevelt.

Payton raised Helen's hand to his lips and kissed the back softly. "Your phenomenal First Lady has chosen to stand by my side. Without her prayers and faithfulness, I would not be alive. God has truly blessed me with a woman of character and grace. Some of you will choose to remain, and some will not. For those of you who do, I promise you this. The Lord will restore us according to His word in Ezekiel 36 Chapter."

Payton paused to keep his composure. "Saints, although I didn't deserve it, the Lord spared my life. So, for the rest of my life, I will strive to live it according to His purpose.

"Look around you for a moment. Thank God that we," he held up their intertwined hands, "the church, his bride, will make it through the storm. Most of us will make it on broken pieces. However, we will make it because His mercy endures forever. May we always be reminded that we, you and I, are the Sanctuary.

"We will build another edifice. But what's in here," pointing to his heart, "that's what matters to God." Pastor Roosevelt held their intertwined hands high and bellowed, "For the saints of God and for the Lamb." The church repeated with a thunderous voice, "For the saints of God and for the Lamb."

Darlene Grant is a dedicated servant to the wholeness and wellbeing of women. She has been involved in ministry since age 9. She is a wife and mother of four. Her life's goal is to comfort them that mourn, give beauty for ashes, the oil of joy for mourning, and the garment of praise for the spirit of heaviness.........
THAT THEY MIGHT LIVE!

www.ingramcontent.com/pod-product-compliance
Lightning Source LLC
LaVergne TN
LVHW051231080426
835513LV00016B/1518